Innovative Apartment Buildings

High Park, San Pedro Garza García, Mexico (see pp. 74–77).

Avi Friedman

Innovative Apartment Buildings
New Directions in Sustainable Design

Edition Axel Menges

© 2017 Edition Axel Menges, Stuttgart/London
ISBN 978-3-86905-009-6

Printing and binding: Graspo CZ, a.s., Zlín, Czech
Republic

Design: Axel Menges
Cover: 625 Rhode Island Avenue, Washington, D.C.,
USA (pp. 70–73). Photo: Alan Karchmer

Acknowledgements

Housing design was the focus of my work for many years. It included collaboration with numerous colleagues, assistants and students who directly and indirectly inspired the generation of the ideas expressed here. In particular I would like to thank Dave Cameron, Emma Greer, Patricia Johnsson, Thi Ngoc Diem Nguyen and Linda Zhang for their help in background research for this book. My apology if I have mistakenly omitted the name of someone who contributed to the ideas or the text that have been included in this book. I will do my best to correct an omission in future editions.

Alexander Bove played a key role in finding the outstanding projects listed here and describing them. His dedication, hard work and interest in the subject are much appreciated.

I would like to express my gratitude to Dorothea Duwe and Axel Menges at Edition Axel Menges GmbH for trust, ushering in the book in and for their patience and guidance in seeing it through.

Thanks to the McGill University's School of Architecture where the genesis of the ideas expressed here and my own research was carried out.

Finally, my heartfelt thanks and appreciation to my wife Sorel Friedman, Ph.D., and children Paloma and Ben for their love and support.

Avi Friedman

Sonnenhof, Jena, Germany (see pp. 56–59).

Contents

The evolution of and current trends in apartment-building design

In many nations a »perfect storm« of social factors has led policy makers, designers and builders to rethink the planning of communities and the design of dwellings. The overarching motive that underlines these initiatives is a need to establish a built environment with small ecological and carbon footprints. Apartment buildings suit this ideological framework well since by the nature of their design more inhabitants reside in one place. Whereas the concept of many households living in a single multi-level structure dates back centuries, this building's form has evolved to respond to emerging realities. An historical chronology of some of these factors as well as contemporary trends and their effect on the design and construction of apartment buildings are described in this chapter.

A study of urban forms demonstrates that apartment buildings were built primarily in cities. The rationale for building tall structures and placing a number of units on top of each other was rooted primarily in a lack of land, which was often imposed by defence walls. Whereas in cities the wealthy commonly resided in townhouses or palaces, the lower classes rented units in crowded apartment buildings. The remains of such places can be seen in Ostia Antica, ancient Rome's port city. For example a building called Insulea stood five to six storeys tall with several Cenaculas windowless units, each containingone or two rooms that measured 20 m² (215 sq. ft.) on each floor. The structure had poor sanitary facilities and ground floor shops facing highly traveled streets. Other civilizations, most notably the Egyptians, also constructed apartment buildings to house urban dwellers.

However it can generally be argued that in the centuries that followed, at least in the western world, apartment buildings were not the primary dwelling type. During the Middle Ages urban dwellers resided primarily in townhouses or lived in the home of the upper class family that they served. After London's Great Fire of 1666, a series of building acts brought uniformity into their construction and they were classified into several categories based on their width and height. Also, various regulations introduced improvements to the manner in which they were constructed to make them safer.

In Paris by the end of the nineteen century the popularity of apartment buildings rose as a result of urban transformation after the redevelopment by Baron Georges-Eugène Haussmann when land for the building of townhouses became prohibitively expensive. Another reason was the urban settings that saw apartment buildings constructed along newly created treed boulevards. The structures boasted palatial façades and offered generously sized rooms, which made them attractive to upper classes. The success of Parisian apartment building as a housing form for upper classes spread to other European hubs like Berlin and Vienna.

Across the Atlantic apartment buildings were introduced in American cities, most notably in New York. It became a housing alternative to the townhouse which formerly housed middle and

1. Ruins of apartment buildings in Ostia Antica near Rome, Italy. A building called Insulea stood five to six storeys tall with several Cenaculas windowless units, each containing one or two rooms that measured 20 m² (215 sq. ft.).

upper class families. The design of the building was influenced by the French prototype noted above. Luxury apartments had doormen, spacious and elegant lobbies, grand staircase and often a clerk's office. The Stuyvesant Building which was designed by Richard Morris Hunt, a Paris-trained American architect, had such features. At first, the building did not gain much popularity with renters due the lack of privacy that the townhouse offered. However this changed with time. The layout of each unit featured several rooms off a long corridor which to some degree limited the units' internal flexibility. The top attic units contained several studio apartments that often attracted artists. Following the market's acceptance of the Stuyvesant Apartment similarly styled buildings were constructed in other highly populated American cities.

Perhaps the one of the most intriguing aspects of apartment building design was that with some modification it could house upper, middle and lower classes. Both in Europe and America the building housed migrants that flocked from the countryside to cities during the Industrial Revolution in search of employment, and in later years immigrants who arrive from other countries. The living conditions in buildings that housed lower classes were in most cases horrific, with entire families often residing in a single room with poor ventilation, no running water and appalling sanitary conditions, a breeding ground for widespread disease. Some apartment buildings were constructed as tenements in proximity to manufacturing plants by factory owners. These were small units in which large families congregated and where bathrooms were public.

The poor living conditions of the masses initiated calls for social reform. Some reformers drew schemes that offered urban planning solutions and designs featuring apartment buildings such as Ebenezer Howard's Garden City in England. Two other earliest reformers were Robert Owen and Charles Fourier of England and France, respectively. In an attempt to alleviate the misery of urban dwellers, both envisioned an ideal city form that would remove the working class from the existing cluttered cities to new developments, structured around a single industry and agriculture. Owen's city, proposed in 1816, was New Lanark, where, in a repeatable square module approximately 1,200 people could reside. Housing enclosed a common space. Communal and recreational buildings were located in the public square, while allotment gardens were placed behind the houses. Though industry was pushed to the periphery of such a development, it should be noted that Owen was a leading industrialist in England, and he therefore provided for a close living relationship to the places of work and for the retention of industry by private interests. In fact, Owen's model town could be considered a benevolent dictatorship, as he specified not only the town form but also the hygienic and virtuous manner in which inhabitants should live.

Fourier created a socialist version of roughly the same type of development. Influenced by the French Revolution and desiring to remove the unemployed from the harsh city environment, he proposed the relocation of society into »phalanxes«. These were single buildings that could house up to 1,600 people in private apartments. Each phalanstery had centralized communal amenities and was situated on a plot of approximately 2,023 hectares (5,000 acres) of land that residents were expected to cultivate, thereby ensuring self-sustenance. Though the socialist foundation of such a design was never realized, the palatial treatment of the architecture was realized at Guise, France.

The realization that poor living conditions put entire cities at risk led to political reform that altered the lives of lower classes and the design of apartment buildings. In 1902 the »Housing Act« was introduced in the Netherlands. The act made it possible to acquire government funds for the development of social housing. The initiative saw dramatic improvements in the type of buildings constructed but more so, the active interest and participation of the state in the well-being of the population. Apartment estates were built by socialist-led city governments or by private investors who took advantage of the grants offered. Having a measure of control over the finances also implied a measure of control over the design. Regulation about the number of units to be served by each stairwell, size of rooms and the amount of light to enter each dwelling were some of the guidelines that were put in place.

Several housing schemes were built in Europe along these ideology and principles. Karl Marx Hof was designed by Karl Ehn and built in Vienna in 1926 with a denser, more urban form surrounding an interior courtyard. The project ran almost a kilometer long and was made of rectilinear blocks four storeys tall and approximately 11 m (36 ft.) deep. The scheme had a total of 1,382 mostly small dwellings with one or two bedrooms, a kitchen and bathroom overlooking either the street or the courtyard.

A project similar in nature was Berlin's Britz Hufeisensiedlung which was designed by Bruno Taut in 1925. It was developed as part of a program to provide much needed housing for workers. Taut's idea was a combination of Ebenezer Howard's Garden City and simple functional plan-

2. A view of Robert Owen's New Lanark Community in Scotland.
3. Karl Marx Hof was built in Vienna in 1926 with a denser urban form surrounding an inner courtyard.
4. Habitat 67 in Montreal attempted to challenge the traditional rectangular apartment block's form.

ning. The 1,000 unit project had two building types, one of which was a three storey apartment building. The units had living space with loggias or balconies on the garden side and access landing and staircases on the opposite side. Several large scale similar housing schemes were built in Europe at the time. By the nature of their design they popularized apartment buildings and established a sense of community and ownership that has stood the test of time.

The next era in apartment building innovation took place after World War II. The reconstruction effort of many European cities and the need to house waves of immigrants and clear poor pre-war districts in America sparked modernization initiatives. Many of the projects were highly monotonous, but among them there those that set the tone for future projects. Such a project was Le Corbusier's Unité d'habitation in Marseille, France. It embodied the architect's own writing and theories and the modernist ideas and vision of how should the inhabitants live. The eighteen-storey block had 337 apartments of 23 different types. The reduced personal space was replaced with communal living area to support family life. Bedrooms and private spaces were minimized to make more room for kitchen andliving areas. Most of the long units enjoyed cross ventilation and views from two façades.

The design of post-World War II East European apartment buildings on the other hand lacked stylistic and architectural diversity. The projects embodied socialist realism with large rectangular structures framing public spaces. Planning initiatives saw entire communities designed based on American Clarence Arthur Perry's neighborhood unit principles with a school as the defining yardstick and apartment buildings facing wide boulevards. Such principles were embedded in the Nowa Huta near Krakow, Poland, a new town for 200,000 inhabitants that was built in the 1950's.

Concerns about a lack of personalization in apartment building design led to calls for giving inhabitants greater choice and say in shaping their dwellings. John Habraken, a Dutch architect, devised a system to assist with such initiative. The essence of Habraken's theory is that the role of the community and the role of the individual in housing are distinct. When we confuse or fail to separate them, the result is the perfect barracks of mass housing. The basic expression of the theory is seen as a dual form of construction, in which supports are permanent, long life, multi-storey artificial land providing utilities and communal services. The dwelling within the supports is formed of what Habraken calls detachable units (e.g. external walls, bathrooms, kitchens, partitions) which should be available to occupants, eventually through normal marketing channels but until then as products of individual manufacturers.

A project that used Habraken's theory to offer maximum choice and scope for participation by users was in Hollabrunn, Austria. The design, a government initiated project, fully applied the hierarchical principle by separating between the structure and the infill. Concrete structures of column and slab were used in a module of 510 by 960 cm (200 by 378 in), and a tartan grid 10 by 20 cm (4 by 7.8 in) was used for the interior arrangement of material and spaces. The inherent openness of the support structure was utilized quite efficiently by the users while achieving floor plans that responded to their needs. A review of the plans and façade demonstrates the uniqueness of each.

Another architect whose ideological departure was also based on a desire to break away from the ubiquitous rectangular apartment block was Moshe Safdie. In Habitat that was built for the 1967 world exhibition in Montreal, he explored the application of modern technology and especially mass production. Laid in a striking fashion, concrete boxes measuring 11.7 m long by 5.3 m wide and 3 m high (38.5 by 17.5 by 10 ft.) incorporated a one piece moulded fiberglass bathroom unit. Despite the fact that the idea was never replicated in another location, it was a unique and creative demonstration of alternative arrangement of units in an apartment building.

The decades that followed World War II saw the introduction of several projects that like Habitat attempted to challenge the traditional rectangular apartment block's form. The 1964 circular Marina City Tower in Chicago by architect Bertrand Goldberg explored new high density living form. The 1971 Nagakin Capsule Tower by Kisho Kurokawa in Tokyo followed the ideology of the Japanese Metabolist Group. The building had pods attached to a core that housed stairs and elevators. Ricardo Bofill's 1974 Walden 7 in Barcelona introduced a new kind of urban living where the units could accommodate offices and shops faced open areas.

The 1980s witnessed several attempts to offer new stylistic exterior ideas. The Atlantis Condominium in Miami, Florida by Architectonica had a Post-Modern expression. To a simple rectangular shape, the architects introduced playful interventions such as red triangle roof, yellow triangle balconies and a »sky court« to create a unique sculptural effect. Another notable project of the same era was the Byker Wall project in Newcastle-upon-Tyne, UK by Ralph Erskine and Vernon Garacie & Associates. Built as a long wall that sheltered behind it two-storey wood-frame single-family housing, it was valued not only for its architectural expression, but for involving the residents in determining the form and function of their own community through ongoing consultation.

The decades that preceded and followed the twenty-first century introduced new social challenges and required innovative solutions that are listed in the various chapters of this book. On a macro level, the need to halt urban sprawl in some countries and rapid urbanization in others has led to increased density of cities around the world. Housing larger number of citizens while reducing a place's carbon and ecological footprints has made apartment buildings a natural housing solution. Be it new construction or conversion of existing structures no longer in use to residences, apartment buildings seem to have gain renewed importance as a result.

Heightened awareness of and the need to respond to the negative effect of global warming shifted architectural priorities to some degree. Designers have begun to reconsider different approaches and include new technologies in their designs. Reducing consumption of non-renewable natural resources such as fossil fuels and freshwater to name a few, has led to energy-efficient construction, net-zero design, passive solar gain strategies, active power generating systems such as photovoltaic panels and water harvesting and recycling methods. Technologies that only years ago were considered marginal are gradually becoming common.

Several notable projects that made energy-saving and the use of renewable power a central theme are featured in chapters 2 (pp. 31–44) and 8 (pp. 137–154). One such project, the BedZed community near London, UK, designed by ZED Factory and include a net-zero apartment buildings which were designed to consume as much as energy as it produced. The project included other environmental related strategies and technologies such as choice of products made of renewable materials and water harvesting and recycled methods.

Having sustainable communities or buildings with multiple land uses or functions is regarded by urban planners to be vital to supporting public transit which result in reduced use of private vehicles and lower carbon dioxide emissions, a leading cause of global warming. Several apartment building designs include a range of functions in their schemes and are outlined in chapter 3 (pp. 45–64). The project, Linked Hybrid, by architect Steven Hall in Beijing, is made of several tall structures connected by sky passes. The design combines functions such as shops, school, hotel, restaurant and cinema to create a self-contained multifunctional urban environment.

Designing buildings while keeping in mind the social needs of the occupants has also taken center stage in recent years. Having outdoor areas and indoor meeting places where people can congregate is known to contribute to the occupants' well-being and mental health and are featured in chapter 4 (pp. 65–86). The 60 Richmond Cooperative Housing in Toronto by the firm Teeple Architects was designed to address the need of lower income buyers and include above

ground outdoor green spaces. In addition to including number of cost reduction strategies, the project features several passive and active environmental innovations.

It can be argued that the »greenest« building is the one that is already built, summarizing the notion that heritage conservation and sustainability are intricately linked. Indeed, preserving and reusing old buildings benefits the environment more than constructing new structures. The process consumes less energy and prevents urban sprawl with the end result of reducing greenhouse gas emissions. Old buildings also define the character of places, and may in turn satisfy the psychological needs of citizens who search for a meaning and identity in their surroundings. People will feel a greater sense of connection to their place of living through a shared history. Such projects have been described in chapter 5 (pp. 87–100).

In addition to social and environmental factors, recent developments in construction methods and technologies also saw rapid evolution in recent decades to affect apartment buildings' design. On a macro level, and in the interest of saving time and money, prefabrication has become more common and accepted around the world. The use of sustainable technologies led to the introduction and use of green roof and products made of recycled materials to name a few. In the interior, novel ways to integrate utilities and make them more efficient and affordable are also included. Such approaches are outlined in chapter 6 (pp. 101–118).

Demographic changes have altered the population of many societies, primarily in western countries. The transformation saw the rise of the non-traditional household to include single and single-parent families. Those households are often looking for units in the heart of cities in proximity to jobs, amenities and public transit. Apartment buildings with a mix of unit types that draw wider range of buyers' types are sought after by these population groups, which explain the rising interest in their construction.

The 8House project in Copenhagen by the Danish firm BIG was designed to offer variety of units in a rather unusual form for an apartment building. Modeled after the number 8 it creates two large outdoor open areas and includes a mix of unit types to form a 3-dimentional neighborhood. There are ground related units, conventional off-central corridor apartments and townhouses. The striking feature of the design is a path along the building's perimeter through which the inhabitants can reach their upper level units by walking or cycling.

Another demographic group whose number is on the rise is seniors. Elderly citizens are projected to make significant share of the population of many nations to occupy the minds of policymakers, architects and the housing industry. It is highly unlikely that housing solutions in institutional affordable assistant living will be common and available for all. Therefore, many seniors will likely age in their own places, some of which will be specially adapted apartments where they will live as long as they can. Another type of projects whose number is likely to rise is apartment buildings for several generations of the same family. The units will offer private and common spaces within the same area to all members of the households. Such designs have been featured in chapter 7 (pp. 119–136).

Another growing phenomenon that has affected apartment building design was the outcome of the digital revolution. The rise of telecommuting and the popularity of live-work arrangements are known to have economic, environmental and social advantages where people can deduct their work-related expenses from their taxes, drive less and have more leisure time. The need for buildings with units that combine live-work functions are expected to further grow in the coming years and are featured in chapter 9 (pp. 155–168).

Economic realities have become another motive for the construction of apartment buildings. Lower incomes, a lack of job security and the high cost of single-family dwellings have made apartment units the only affordable housing solution in many nations. In this regard it seems that first time North American buyers are closing ranks with their European and Asian counterparts. High costs coupled with lifestyle and demographic transformations have led to the introduction of very small dwellings known as micro units and flexible interiors, which are featured in chapter 10 (pp. 169–185). Throughout history designers of apartment buildings have displayed a remarkable ability to modify this housing form according to ongoing circumstances. Our era is no different. Contemporary social challenges require architects to be innovative in their responses. It is also likely that in coming years new challenges may lead to other design approaches. The trends outlined in this book and resulting architectural responses are a demonstration that the design and construction of apartment buildings will continue to evolve and endure.

5. Linked Hybrid in Beijing combines functions such as shops, school, hotel, restaurant and cinema to create a self-contained multifunctional urban environment.
6. 8House in Copenhagen was designed to offer variety of units in a rather unusual form. Modeled after the number 8, it creates two large outdoor open areas and includes a mix of unit types to form a three-dimensional neighborhood.

Villiot-Râpée apartments, Paris, France
Design: Hamonic Masson & Associés, 2011

The Villiot Râpée apartments are located in Paris near the Gare de Lyon business district. The project consists of two buildings one eleven storeys and the other eight with a total of 62 units. Both buildings have a combined area of 5,120 m² (55,111 sq. ft.).

When coordinating the renewal of these two apartment blocks, the designers aimed at creating a connection between them, enhancing the buildings' green features and adding vibrancy to the district. To establish a physical link, they add a sense of motion to the duo by joining them with an arc-shaped path.

The designers also considered that the complex is in close proximity to the city center when incorporating green features, especially since the city of Paris enforces a strict energy code. Therefore, the goal was to assist the occupants' reduce their energy consumption. Although both blocks are quite tall, many windows allow for an abundance of natural light to penetrate, thereby reducing the residents' need for artificial light. Another design decision that stemmed from the site's location near the city center was the use of soundproof materials. In addition, the buildings have green roofs and photovoltaic (PV) panels and the entire site is landscaped with gardens filled with plants and trees.

The architects' selection of building materials also amplifies the green features as well as defines each unit. Since both buildings consist of hybrid shapes made off steel and aluminum, the use of interesting screen walls and balustrades between each deck prevents residents from seeing into each other's quarters to enhance privacy. Most importantly, the colored steel and aluminum panels along the façades deflect sunlight from the buildings, while the colored glass panels let in just enough light to provide the private terraces with shade and warmth. The stark contrast between the white ceilings in the apartments and the silver-colored gangway ceilings above the private terraces offer a gentle reminder of the division between interior and exterior.

The Villiot Râpée apartments provide a vision of what modern apartment architecture could be. It offers a combination of novel materials, colored accents, green spaces, and fluid shapes which all seek to enhance privacy, vibrancy, and energy efficiency. The complex's conscientious and aspiring design was recognized with Qualitel – the French High Quality Environmental certification.

1. Site plan showing the two buildings that make up the project in their urban context. The designers considered the complex's proximity to the city center when incorporating green features, especially since the city of Paris enforces a strict energy code.
2. A view of the two buildings. When coordinating the renewal of these two apartment blocks, the designers aimed at creating a connection between them, enhancing the buildings' green features and adding vibrancy to the district.

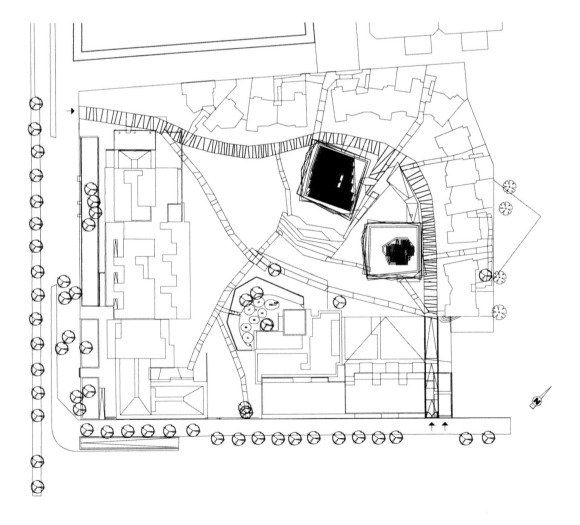

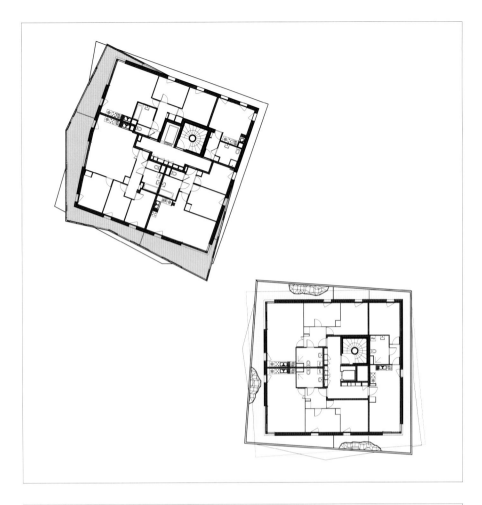

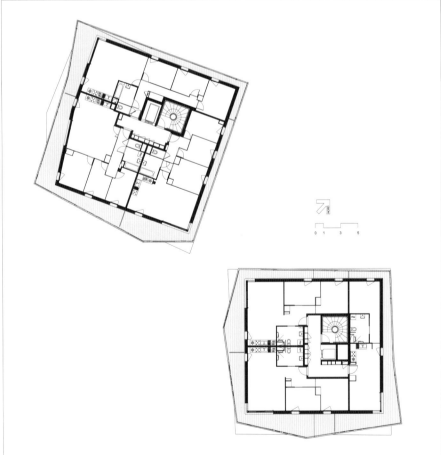

3–6. Floor plans (two typical upper floors of both buildings with each room having access to an outside balcony).

7. Section through one of the buildings and an elevation of the other. Both blocks are quite tall, yet the many windows allow for an abundance of natural light to penetrate, thereby reducing the residents' need for artificial light.

8. A view from an upper floor room onto a terrace.

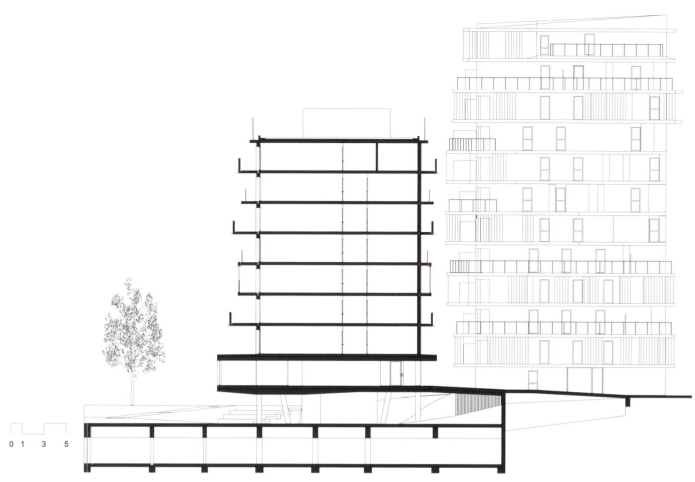

0 1 3 5

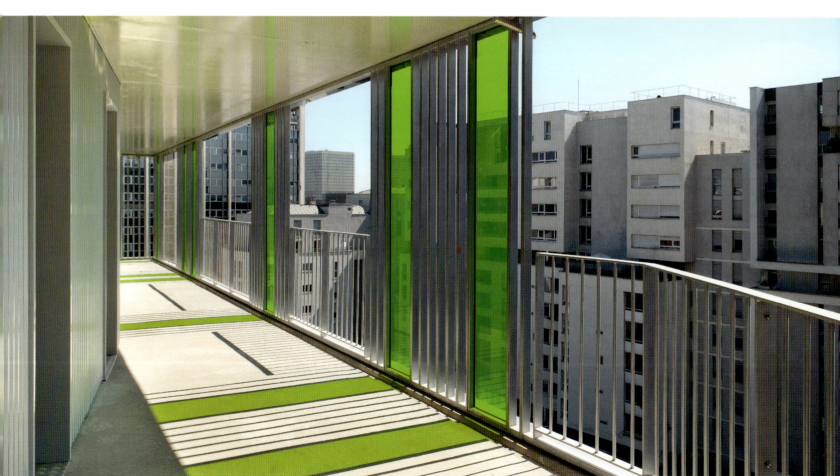

Biscornet apartment building, Paris, France

Design: [BP] Architectures Jean Bocabeille et Ignacio Prego, 2011

The Biscornet apartment building in Paris has an attractive design that fit well in the urban fabric. The project is located near a canal, while also offering a view towards the nearby Gare de Lyon business district and has a footprint of approximately 1,609 m² (17,319 sq. ft.).

Contrary to other apartment buildings near the city center, the architects wanted the design to embody some of the common traits to Parisian architecture. At the same time, they also sought out to design a building that would comply with the strict energy code imposed by the city. The building sits in the intersection of two streets with views of Place de la Bastille. Consequently, designers opted to suggest a façade made entirely of windows to maximize views onto the Place. However, these windows are far from ordinary. If one looks closely, the entire façade is composed of horizontal segments of glass shutters. These shutters are operated by the occupants which lets them control the amount of sunlight that penetrates in. In addition, the glass used for these shutters contains an amber tint, which offers additional protection from sunlight, as well as privacy when the shutters are closed. When all the window shutters are closed, people walking along Rue de Lyon see an entirely unified glass façade.

In regard to materials, the use of iron, aluminum, concrete, and glass helped the structure fit nicely into the urban fabric. Also, the choice of materials employed on the other façades consists of side blocks clad in golden aluminum panels, whose angular relief meant to create a unique effect when light shines on them. Throughout the entire building, the window frames are composed of exuberant colors: pink, mauve and orange that are quite visible along both street side façades. They are also conveniently embedded in the glass window shutter façade. Furthermore, when the window shutters are open, flashes of these eccentric pink, mauve and orange colors can be seen.

Through the use of particular materials and shapes, the designers were able to fulfill their goal and design an apartment building, which responds appropriately to its trapezoidal plot of land. In addition, they created a magnificent structure, which considers energy efficiency and whose building materials exercise an intriguing relationship with sun and night lights.

1. Street view. The building sits at the intersection of two streets with views of Place de la Bastille.
2, 3. Floor plans (residential floors, top) and a floor used as office space on another level, bottom).
4. The site plan shows the proximity of the building to Opera de la Bastille.

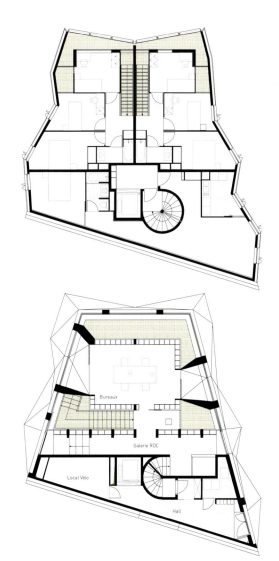

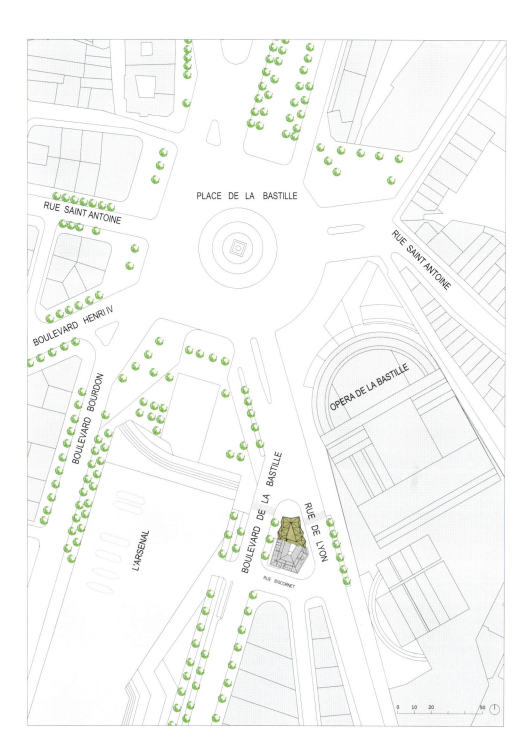

RUE SAINT ANTOINE

PLACE DE LA BASTILLE

RUE SAINT ANTOINE

BOULEVARD HENRI IV

OPERA DE LA BASTILLE

BOULEVARD BOURDON

BOULEVARD DE LA BASTILLE

RUE DE LYON

L'ARSENAL

RUE BISCORNET

Bureaux

Galerie RDC

Local Vélo

Hall

0   10   20   50

5. Side view showing the shutters which let the occupants control the amount of sunlight that penetrates into the apartment.
6. Section showing above and underground floor levels.
7. One of the units' interiors showing work, living and kitchen spaces.

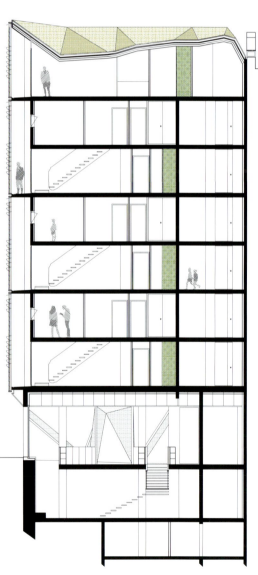

On the Corner, Higashiomi, Japan
Design: Eastern Design Office, 2009

On the Corner is an apartment complex whose designers faced a challenging location. The building houses seven units with a floor area of 567 m² (6,103 sq. ft.). The site is triangular, with an acute angle on one corner, resulting from an intersection of two streets. The architect in charge was asked to rethink common ideas and themes usually seen in apartment buildings for this design to be realized. The main focus was to highlight the shape of the lot, which were previously regarded as unfavorable and void. Therefore, the form of the structure takes the shape of a triangular wedge, a direct reflection of the plot's actual form. The complex measures 13 m (43 ft.) tall with base lines of 23 m (75 ft.) and 26 m (85 ft.).

When considering the plan layout of the units each apartment has a living room, two bedrooms, a prefabricated bathroom, and a kitchen. It is also important to note that the designers efficiently utilize all of the available space provided by the plot's shape which made the units favorable by renters.

In addition to their innovative spatial organization, the architects have selected interesting materials and forms to enhance the appearance of the building. Despite the striking triangular structure, Eastern Design Office opted to employ rectilinear forms and orthogonal lines along the façades. The building was fabricated using reinforced concrete and the exterior wall features square shaped stone, concrete and glass. These three materials used on the outermost layer of the envelope are used intermediately. The lines and planes formed along the façades by the scattered building materials are enhanced by their naturally sharp edges.

On the Corner represents a striking architectural response to the spatial constraints imposed by the site. Furthermore, the architects' ability to surmount the barriers of conventional apartment building design when adapting the plan layout, building materials, and forms of On the Corner made this building very attractive.

1. The building was constructed in the heart of an established urban area. The main planning focus was to highlight the shape of the lot, which was previously regarded as unfavorable and void.
2. The site is triangular, with an acute angle on one corner, resulting from the intersection of two streets.
3. The structure has the shape of a triangular wedge, a direct reflection of the plot's form.

scale=1:1,500

SITE

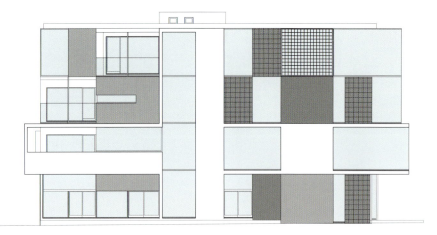

4. The designers opted to employ rectilinear forms and orthogonal lines along the façades, as demonstrated in this elevation.

5, 6. The designers efficiently utilized all of the available space that was dictated by the plot's shape, as shown in these floor plans.

7. The building was prefabricated using reinforced concrete panels, and the exterior features square shaped stone, concrete and glass.

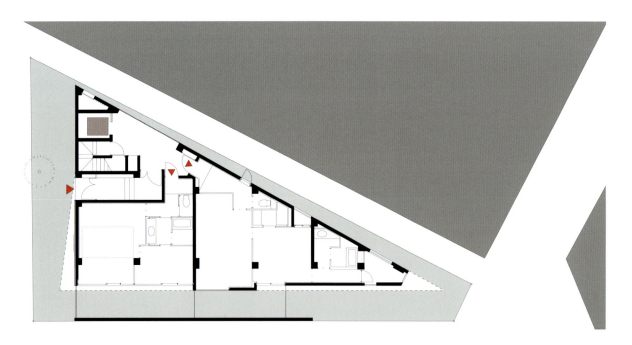

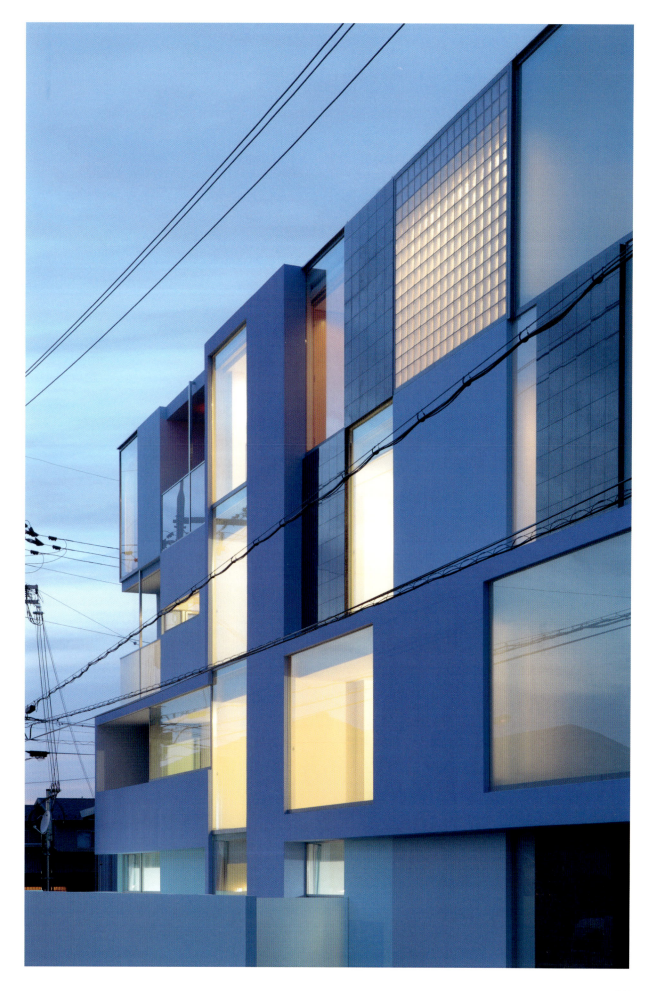

Residence building, Cessange, Luxembourg
Design: METAFORM atelier d'architecture, 2011

The Residence building occupies a small narrow plot in a suburban sector of Cessange, Luxembourg and house four units on four floors. One of the project's goals was to combined design and artistic features and produce fusion between architecture and graffiti art.

The first floor contains a 80 m² (861 sq. ft.) two-bedroom apartment, while the second floor accommodates two studio units. The third and fourth floors include of a duplex apartment split across both levels. To realize their goal, the architects paired up with a local artist name SUMO, who was actively involved in the interior design of each unit, as well as the artistic representations on the façades. The decision to involve a graffiti artist was to reflect the evolution of the urban landscape, known as the post-graffiti era.

In essence, the design of the building can be defined as multiple overhanging volumes. The underside of these very contemporary overhanging shapes was covered with yellow, orange and red graffiti clouds. This exuberant color pallet was also used on the background of the exterior loggias. As for the underlying structure of the building, concrete and aluminum were used as predominant building materials while the façades were composed of black shiny extruded metal. In this case, the architects decided to utilize a single building material to enact the monolithic and sculptural shapes present in the structure. SUMO's artistic contributions on the underside of the overhanging volumes provided a formal distinction between the ground floor, upper floors and the roof. Black shiny extruded metal, coupled with the eccentric color pallet selected by the artist were intended to highlight the Residence building and illustrate that it is very different from its neighbors. The nature of the extruded metal was also employed to provide sharp contrast with its neighbors. On a sunny day, the exterior envelope of the building reflects warm, intense color due to the metallic materials, while the plaster façades of neighboring buildings provide a dull, absorbing effect.

In addition to their quest to depict fusion between art and architecture, the designers kept in mind energy-efficiency. The façades include extruded metal panels which can be moved to act as screens at the residents' discretion. This performs as both a control of sunlight and nightlight into the apartment and a mode of enhancing privacy. In addition, a partial green roof was incorporated and the architects implemented a rainwater recovery system to supply it.

1. The design of the Residence building can be regarded as multiple overhanging volumes, as shown in this view.
2. The ground floor plan demonstrates the building's small footprint which leaves room for green areas.
3–6. Floor plans. The first floor contains a two-bedroom apartment, while the second floor accommodates two studio units. The third and fourth floors include of a duplex apartment split across both levels.

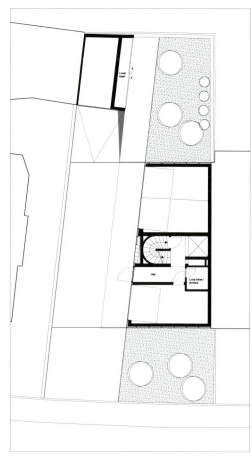

Living area

Loggia

Sleeping area

Kitchen

Apartment 02
48.00 m²

Bathroom

Bathroom

Kitchen

Apartment 03
47.65 m²

Living area

Sleeping area

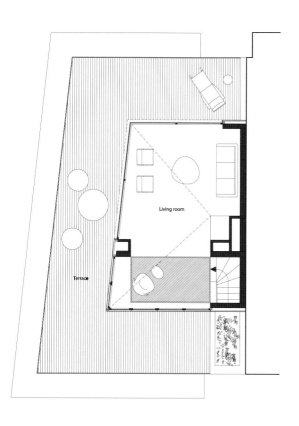

Living room

Terrace

Bedroom 1

Bedroom 2

Bathroom

WC

Apartment 01
78.00 m²

Kitchen

Living/Dining room

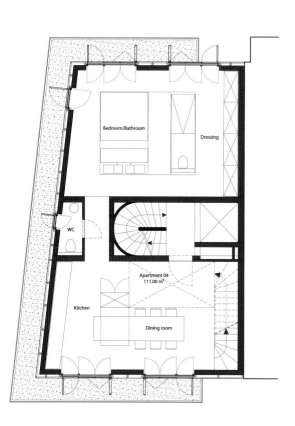

Bedroom/Bathroom

Dressing

WC

Apartment 04
111.00 m²

Kitchen

Dining room

7. The structure of the building is made up of concrete and aluminum while the façades were composed of black shiny extruded metal.
8. A view of a bedroom.
9. The open-plan concept of the interior combines kitchen, dining, and living spaces.

Net-zero buildings

Climate change and dwindling reserves of fossil fuels are forcing us to re-evaluate traditional ways of harvesting and consuming energy. It also heighten the need for a new approaches to architectural design. Net-zero buildings are capable of producing renewable energy equal to the amount of their annual consumption. This chapter explores apartment buildings that are constructed in an energy-efficient manner and that obtain their power supply primarily from on-site sources. When designing a net-zero building an important factor to consider are its heating and cooling systems. Since the energy consumed by a building's mechanical systems accounts for around 55 percent of the structure's overall energy consumption, net-zero apartments need to include other strategies. Principles such as better envelope insulation, wastewater heat recovery, higher quality windows, natural ventilation, green roofs and thermal mass contribute to improved performance as much as, if not more than, the mechanical systems themselves.

Another principle of net-zero building is their energy production method. It is important to decide whether the building will be off-grid – using batteries to store energy for low production times – or grid-tied – in which case the structure can draw from and feedback to the local power grid. This decision will affect the type of chosen system and therefore construction cost.

Whether a building is off-grid or grid-tied, to qualify as net-zero, it cannot emit any carbon dioxide. Although this immediately rules out the use of fossil fuel furnaces, there are still many applicable systems such as photovoltaic panels and wind turbines to choose from. Furthermore, it is best to combine these electricity production avenues with other heat generation methods such as geothermal pumps and solar hot water vacuum tubes. While such heat production systems do not actually produce electricity, they are valuable in reducing the amount required to heat the building, making electricity production more effective.

There exists a range of energy sources for net-zero buildings including solar collection, wind power, hydroelectric power, geothermal energy and biogas. However, not all these means operate at the same scale. Wind power, for example, depends in part on the turbine's efficiency and its size for an optimal output.

Photovoltaic (PV) cells are a common example of active solar technologies suitable for apartment buildings. They are electronic devices, often in the form of panels that can convert solar radiation into electricity. Their output depends on the intensity of solar rays and duration of the sun's heat, therefore their placement on the building's roof or exterior walls with respect to the sun's path and areas of shade are key to their efficiency.

Passive solar design (PSD) includes techniques that take advantage of the sun's heat when it is beneficial and avoids it when it is disadvantageous. These basic principles constitute the most cost effective approach to energy self-sufficient apartment buildings and can reduce heating load significantly in cold climates. Overhang fixtures direct the sun's rays away in the summer while allowing winter sun in at lower angles. As a rule for achieving the best passive solar design, in the northern hemisphere architects should orient major openings toward the south, limit windows on western and eastern elevations and avoid using north facing windows.

Thermal Mass is another aspect that contributes to passive solar design. It is defined as any dense material that stabilizes temperature fluctuations by storing heat when the surroundings are at a higher temperature than the mass, and releasing thermal energy when the surroundings are cooler. The conservation of energy produced on site -making the most out of the available energy-by the aforementioned strategies is an inseparable part of net-zero energy design. Therefore, having a well-built building envelope is an important part of this procedure.

Other opportunities for energy conservation include wastewater heat recovery, energy efficient appliances and smart energy controlling systems. In the latter two cases, greater emphasis is placed on the user to make conscious decisions about how their spend energy. In any case, net-zero and off-the-grid buildings require that designers, builders and occupants be actively engaged in a culture of self-sufficiency.

It is expected that the greatest influence on the advancement of energy-saving techniques will be initiated by designers and organizations. Whether through subsidies or private investments, innovation in energy conserving and storing methods will reduce our impact on the environment and our future energy bills.

BedZed Community, Sutton (London), UK

Design: ZED Factory, 2002

The BedZed Community is one of the first projects in the UK to include apartment buildings with net-zero energy strategies that consume roughly as much power as they produce.

The project showcases eight apartment buildings, most of which are three storeys tall. The location, positioning and shape of the buildings function in parallel with the energy-efficiency and production concepts and site's chosen density. The mixed-used BedZed community includes public, private and semi-private spaces. Each unit has access to a private green space or outdoor area. The planning concept seeks to promote social interaction by creating common areas and public outdoor spaces. Modest bridges cross over public pathways to connect residential units, office spaces and roof terraces.

One of the unique aspects of BedZed is its car-free living. Since the design includes mixed-use buildings, amenities such as kindergarten, fitness center, and offices are all available on site making car ownership redundant. Frequent public transit and bicycle routes offer various methods of commuting the short distances to amenities. In addition, an on-site electric charging station for cars is available, with the capability of charging forty cars at any given time.

The community area covers 12,000 m^2 (129,166 sq. ft.) and integrates different housing styles, including townhouses, two floor (maisonette) and one/two room apartments units. Moreover, the plan layout of the apartments also reflects the energy concept of the community. Interior layout of each module consists of three sections: double-glazed, full-storey patio rooms that serve as thermal buffers located along the southeastern perimeter. This segment is partially shaded by horizontal glazing with integrated solar cells. Other rooms like living and office spaces are located along a northwestern axis, to recive ambient daylight from the north. On the other hand, living rooms are kept warm through southern exposure to sun. The south façade, is almost entirely fenestrated with triple glazed, argon-filled thermal wood frame windows. During construction the architects were environmentally conscientious about choosing building materials. Therefore they selected materials with low embodied energy that were sourced locally to avoid excessive transport.

Energy-efficiency was a key design focus which was reflected in most decisions. Materials such as exposed concrete walls, ceilings, and ceramic tiles floors have a high thermal mass and retain heat. Also, the ventilation system, with a heat recovery ratio of 70 percent, along with an airtight envelope minimized heat loss. Along the roof, the colorful and aesthetically pleasing wind cowls serve as the ventilation system's air intake. Within the apartments, water-saving plumbing fixtures and energy efficient lighting are used to reduce hot water demands and save electricity. BedZed's omnipresent use of photovoltaic cells, which cover an area of 777 m^2 (8,363 sq. ft.), satisfy 15 percent of the community's total power consumption. A state of the art woodchip-fired combined heat and power (CHP) system produces the remainder of the necessary heat and electricity required for the project. The average electricity consumption for the community is 34 kWh/m^2 a while households in the same district were recorded using 48kWh/m^2 a.

In sum, in addition to designing a visually attractive community, ZEDFactory satisfied zero-energy properties. Their objective was successfully achieved as demonstrated by energy consumption of 60 percent less than other residential buildings in the UK.

1. As demonstrated in the site plan, the location, positioning and shape of the buildings in BedZed coincide with the energy-efficiency and passive solar gain objectives of the designers.
2. The project showcases eight apartment buildings, most of which are three storeys tall.

3. Modest bridges cross over public pathways to connect residential units, office spaces and roof terraces to one another.

4. Floor plans. The community integrates different housing types, including townhouses, two-floor (maisonette) and one/two-room apartment units.

5. Section. The interior layout of each module consists of double-glazed, full-storey patio rooms that serve as thermal buffers along the southeastern perimeter.

6. Along the roof, the colorful and aesthetically pleasing wind cowls serve as the ventilation system's air intake.

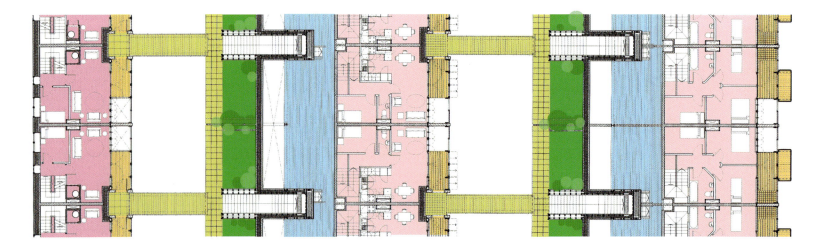

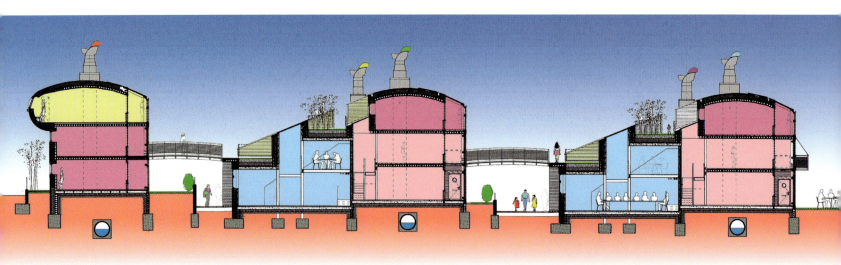

Energy Plus community, Weiz, Austria
Design: Kaltenegger & Partner, 2008

The Energy Plus community consists of 6 small residential blocks, totaling 2,860 m² (30,785 sq. ft.), that features interconnected row houses of different sizes in Austria.

In Austria, net-zero buildings are highly environmentally sensitive. Architects do not only seek to design zero-energy buildings that are self-sufficient, but also make it a requirement to produce surplus energy. Some of the main technologies used to achieve environmental sustainability are photovoltaic cells, and the production of heat via renewable energy sources. The prominence of photovoltaic cells is mainly due to the many green incentives offered by the government regarding energy balance, and the return on surplus energy. Therefore, the Energy Plus community in Weiz, Austria results in a net-zero project that actually produces more energy than it consumes.

The project's photovoltaic systems produce more energy than is required to operate the de-centralized heat-pumps and other electric loads in these all–electric buildings. Despite being very concerned with the environmental sustainability of the building, the architects had certain other conceptual goals that they wanted to achieve. Each of the six row buildings consists of three, four, or five connected structures with two different floor plans (93m² or 105m²). The rows are not strictly orientated towards the south. Instead the architecture is integrated into the landscape in order to create a desired state of harmony between both. The southern orientation of the individual rows varies by 12° to 34°. Some of the other environmental features help contribute to the buildings zero-energy advantage as well. Notably, Energy Plus community is equipped with a de-centralized ventilation system that features heat recovery. Also, the buildings benefit from passive solar gain through south façades, and solar protection via metal sun-breaks above the windows.

The Energy Plus community is an excellent example of a set of interconnected dwelling units that function pragmatically, while satisfying net-zero criteria through their sustainable systems.

1. The Energy Plus community, as demonstrated by the site plan, consists of six small residential blocks that features interconnected row houses of different sizes.

2. Key technologies used to achieve environmental sustainability are photovoltaic cells and the production of heat via renewable energy sources.

3. Each of the six buildings consists of three, four, or five connected structures with two different floor plans.

4, 5. As demonstrated by the floor plans, the units have a simple interior layout.

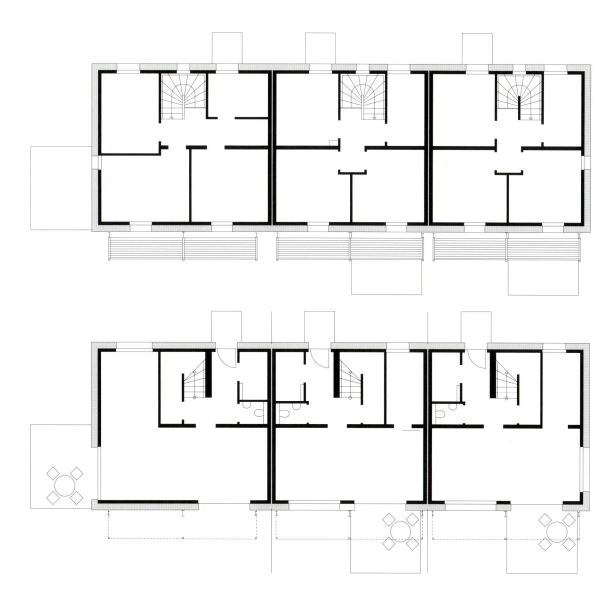

Multi-family dwelling, Dübendorf, Switzerland
Design: kämpfen für architektur ag, 2008

The multi-family dwelling is a 6-unit apartment building in Switzerland, near Zurich, with a total area of 986 m² (10,613 sq. ft.).

This development is situated in a residential neighborhood comprised of small, simple houses with large gardens built during the 1920s and 1930s. In order to increase the occupational density on this accessible site near the Dübendorf city center, the architect and client elected to design a small apartment complex that would serve as a model house in terms of economy and energy. Despite the increased density of the building, it fits in very eloquently with the surrounding urban fabric of the neighborhood. Moreover, a completely glazed stairwell separates the building into two parts and creates a strong visual link between the garden and adjacent street. This glazed stairway serves as a protected circulatory route (albeit unheated) leading to each of the three residential storeys. The southern oriented glazed roof is equipped with vacuum tube collectors that serve as space and water heaters, while providing sun protection. As the sun travels during the day, the collectors result in varying light and shadow panels along the exposed concrete walls, reminding residents of the sustainable features that the building possesses.

The concept of three building segments is easily perceivable from the exterior, and was intended during construction. Both residential cubes are made of prefabricated wood elements while the stairwell features glazed surroundings. The structural independence of each segment improves the building's overall soundproofing. Multi-family dwelling's sustainability also extends to its building materials. Consequently, the lower floor is composed of pre-fabricated hollow members that are built with recycled concrete. Also, the timber utilized in the wall assemblies is pre-fabricated at a carpentry shop prior to on-site delivery. Moreover, this high degree of prefabrication reduces on-site construction time, and improves assembly precision. Taking into consideration its environmental sensitivity, the project follows a passive solar concept and meets MINERGIE-P-ECO certificate requirements, due to very low energy demands based on excellent insulation properties and an airtight building shell.

1. The development, as demonstrated by the site plan, is situated in a neighborhood comprised of small, simple houses.
2. The timber utilized in the wall assemblies was prefabricated prior to site delivery.
3–5. Floor plans (a glazed stairwell separates the building into two parts and creates a strong visual link between the garden and adjacent street).

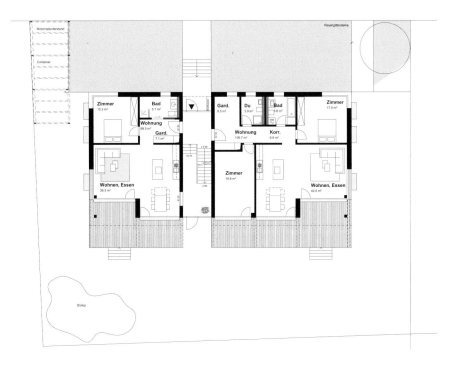

UC Davis West Village, Davis, California, USA
Design: Studio E Architects, 2011

The UC West Davis Village is the largest planned net-zero community in the USA. It covers an area of 4,180 m² (45,000 sq. ft.) adjacent to the core campus of the University of California, Davis.

The goal of the designers was to create a mixed-community that includes student housing, single-family homes, retail spaces, and recreational facilities. In essence, it was designed to enable faculty, staff, and students to reside near the campus, take advantage of environmentally friendly methods of transportation, and participate in campus life. The requirements of this project included 123 units, which consist of student apartments in one, two, and three bedroom layouts. Another objective was for the entire community to satisfy a zero energy criterion. Prior to focusing on the energy-efficiency of each structure, the architects opted to design the layout of the individual buildings to satisfy a certain predetermined program. The buildings were arranged according to scale, allowing for small and large gathering spaces between them. This allows people to stroll, linger and interact, all the while enjoying the outdoors. Once the orientation of the structures was decided, the architects tailored each to function as a sustainable unit of the entire campus.

Although the project looks very similar to existing communities, every design decision sought to emphasize how simple and inexpensive solutions could be implemented to decrease energy consumption. Each building possesses a saw-toothed roof; a unique trait which unifies the whole plan. However, this particular roof shape contributes to the net-zero identity. The tilted roofs are entirely covered with state of the art photovoltaic cells. In addition, their southern orientation maximizes the amount of sunlight that they receive, and in turn, the amount of energy that they can generate. When considering the southern and western façades, the architects chose to employ vertical corrugated steel siding, which are designed to ventilate the walls. This design decision creates a thermal shield along the envelope, protecting the complexes from heat gain from the afternoon sun.

To further protect the buildings from heat, sunshades were specifically oriented along the façades to soften the summer sun's heat, while allowing the lower lighting conditions of winter sun to warm the interior of each unit. Moreover, the southern side of each structure is equipped with deep roof overhangs to minimize heat gain, and optimize the surface area available for photovoltaic cells. The choices of materials in the building envelope also enhance its green features. Inexpensive materials coupled with recyclable entities were used to insulate each structure. Similarly to other net-zero projects, the architects consulted with energy experts, in this case Davis Energy Group, to select appliances and fixtures, which require less energy. This notion is integral in a net-zero community since a building that requires less energy to function will require less energy to be generated by the self-sufficient network.

Studio E Architects and Davis Energy Group's environmentally friendly decisions have helped shape a community which not only produces enough energy to sustain itself, but is also able to sell excess energy back to the grid.

1. The UC Davis West Village is a mixed community that includes student housing, single-family homes, retail spaces, and recreational facilities as seen in this overview.
2. The buildings as shown in this site plan were arranged according to various scales, allowing small and large outdoor spaces for gathering between them.

pp. 42, 43
3, 4. Floor plans of the two building types that include units of various sizes and layouts to accommodate a wide range of inhabitants.
5. The planning concept of the Village created public open spaces where people can stroll and interact while enjoying the outdoors.
6, 7. View of a kitchen and a bedroom.

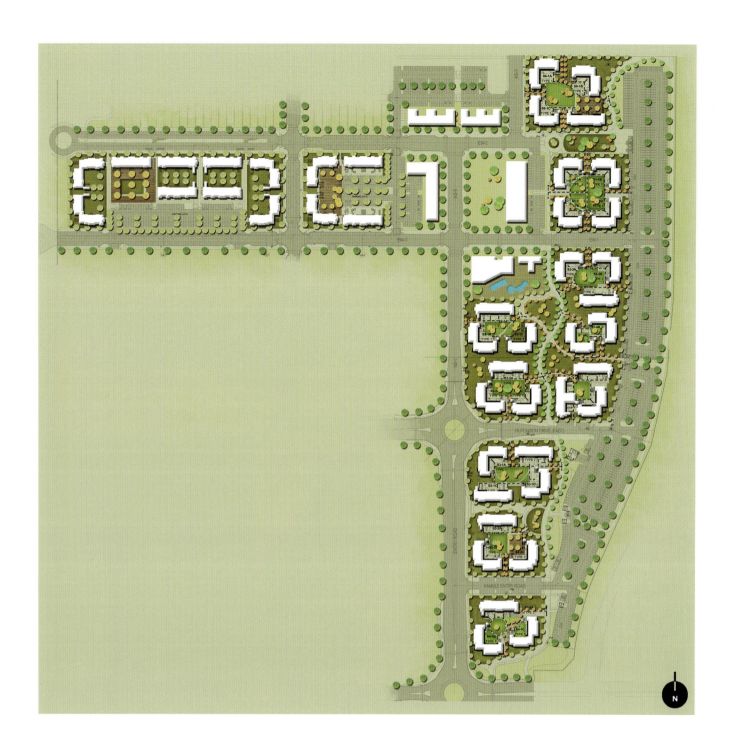

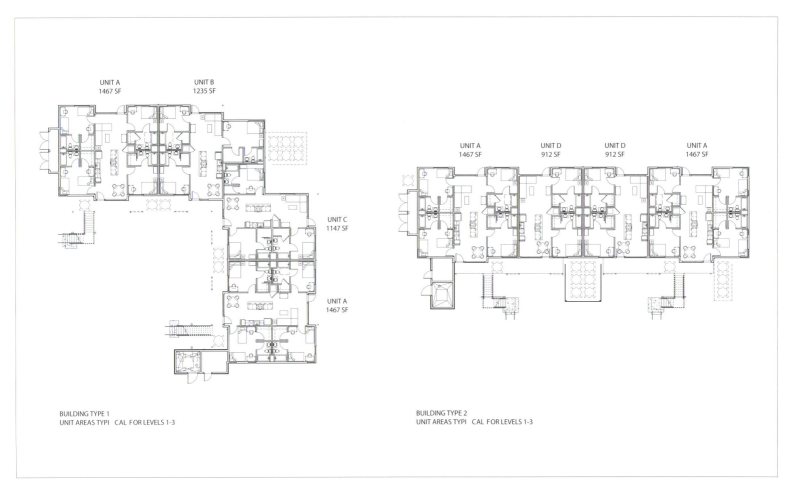

UNIT A
1467 SF

UNIT B
1235 SF

UNIT C
1147 SF

UNIT A
1467 SF

UNIT A
1467 SF

UNIT D
912 SF

UNIT D
912 SF

UNIT A
1467 SF

BUILDING TYPE 1
UNIT AREAS TYPI CAL FOR LEVELS 1-3

BUILDING TYPE 2
UNIT AREAS TYPI CAL FOR LEVELS 1-3

Mixed-use buildings

Planners argue that having a community with mixed land uses can establish sustainable environments that enable less driving. Unlike historic urban patterns many apartment buildings of the latter half of the twentieth century were made up of only dwelling units. When properly designed, activities such as working, shopping, and leisure can take place in the same location. This chapter ses and illustrates designs that combine non-residential activities and housing in the same structure.

Urban sprawl poses a significant challenge to regions dealing with the complexities of metropolitan growth. Peripheral developments force residents to commute long distances to work, shop or study – and create a burdensome demand for highway infrastructure. These challenges can be mitigated by planning communities with mixed-use buildings that can attract diverse populations and businesses. Such buildings are known to contribute to having a wider range of socio-economic groups, build diversity and vibrancy and foster equity by providing affordable housing.

Varieties of design strategies have been suggested in recent years for the reestablishment of sustainable mixed-use buildings. The aim of these concepts is to combine commerce, employment and housing in unique locations and urban contexts. For example, transit-oriented developments (TOD) focus on mixed-use apartment buildings that are constructed near transit corridors or within an easy walking distance from them. Such developments are compact, pedestrian-friendly, and can be customized to offer a wide variety of housing options with convenient access to services and jobs. The size of a commercial center where the buildings are located depends on the area of the neighbourhood. Known as convenience centers they have a mix of amenities such as a daycare, fitness club, beauty salon, or a grocery store, all located under dwellings.

On a macro level, the design challenge is what types of functions are most suitable to mix and where to locate them in the community and the building. For reasons of safety and privacy the non-residential functions need to include non-polluting functions and those that are not causing noise and avoid intrusions onto private property. It is therefore recommended to locate retail-related functions on the ground floor, offices on the second floor and dwellings on the rest of the upper floors.

Another way of creating mixed-use buildings is to form transition nodes. Within this scheme, smaller apartment buildings encircle larger stores, fostering a sense of community and introducing human scale to a retail sector. Organizing commerce in this way reduces traffic congestion and creates an aesthetically pleasing, diverse environment. Taller buildings help create a pleasing microclimate that blocks wind, sheltering pedestrians in cold regions. Further, residences located near or within transition nodes benefit from being nearby amenities to which they can walk. Also, residents and visitors are not subject to the unattractive street façades common to large, isolated shopping malls or big-box retail establishments.

Another practice is the inclusion of very light industry such as microprocessor-manufacturing in buildings. Technological advances have alleviated the environmental concerns associated with the integration of industry into urban areas to avoid pollution. Working near home is seen as a highly sustainable practice as it cuts down on transportation costs and fuel consumption and generates income for working age households.

On a micro level, the commercial floors and residences should have separate entrances. For the parking, the retail can use on-street parking or a specially designated lot at the back and the residents can park underground. Often in dense urban areas municipalities accept the occupants of the residential units will not have parking at all.

In a large structure, civic institutions such as a small library or even medical offices can be integrated with commerce and housing. The building can also include educational functions such as a day care center. The merging of cultural and educational functions will contribute to the benefit of both since they will be in greater use. Those functions should have distinct entrances separating them from each other. The architectural quality of these buildings is also important as they play a valuable community role. They can face or be sited near squares to transform them into hubs.

The buildings can form a convenience center on their own and can help people meet and develop a sense of communal ownership. Such buildings need to be within a short walking distance from other housing to make them functional and be used by elderly people as well.

Linked Hybrid, Beijing, China
Design: Steven Holl Architects, 2009

Linked Hybrid is a large mixed-use development made-up of several linked structures that includes 750 dwelling units with a gross floor area of 220,000 m² (2,152,782 sq. ft.). The goal of the designers was to create a twenty-first century porous urban space that functions as a city within a city due to its multifaceted layers.

Situated on a site adjacent to Beijing's old city wall, the pedestrian oriented development is inviting, walkable and open to the public. Various links or bridges connect each part to the next, essentially redefining the notion of public urban space. It promotes encounters and interactions across realms of commerce, housing, education and leisure. One can consider the development a three-dimensional community where spaces on, above and underground are fused together efficiently.

To further enhance social interactions in the public space, Linked Hybrid's ground level offers foot passages for residents and visitors to create interesting micro-spaces to which the shops around a central reflective pond infuse life. On the intermediate level of some of the buildings, roof gardens offer tranquil green spaces, and at the top of the eight residential towers private green areas are connected to the penthouses. Every ground level public function including Montessori school, a hotel, restaurant, kindergarten and cinema have a clearly defined connection to the green spaces.

The designers integrated an elevator that travels to the sky passages on upper levels. A multi-functional series of sky bridges with a swimming pool, a fitness room, a café, a gallery, auditorium and a mini salon are present from the twelve to the eighteen floors and connect all eight residential towers with the hotel tower. These innovative sky bridges also permit magnificent views of the city. In terms of organization, these interconnected structures aim to be a semi-lattice rather than a simply linear form. Due to the nature of their design the towers function as social condensers, which create a special experience reminiscent of city life for visitors and residents.

In addition to architectural features, Linked Hybrid incorporated environmental aspects and uses geo-thermal energy to cools the project in summer time and provides heat in winter to make it one of the largest green residential projects in the world.

The cutting edge urban design approach makes this project an outstanding development to redefine apartment building estate.

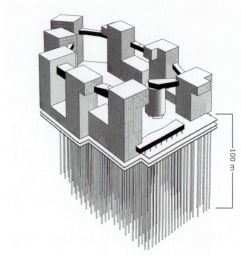

660 GEOTHERMAL WELLS / 100 m DEEP
5000 KW COOLING / HEATING CAPACITY

1. Linked Hybrid is a porous urban space that functions as a city within a city due to its multifaceted layers as demonstrated in this site plan.
2. Linked Hybrid uses geo-thermal energy for cooling and heating to make it one of the largest »green« residential projects in the world.
3. Linked Hybrid is situated adjacent to Beijing's old city wall. The pedestrian-oriented development is inviting, walkable, and open to the public.

pp. 48, 49
4. Linked Hybrid can be regarded as a three-dimensional community where spaces on, above and underground are fused.
5. A section showing the buildings and the open spaces in between.
6. To further enhance social interactions in public spaces, Linked Hybrid's ground level offers foot passages over water to create interesting areas; shops surrounding a central reflective pond infuse life into this space.

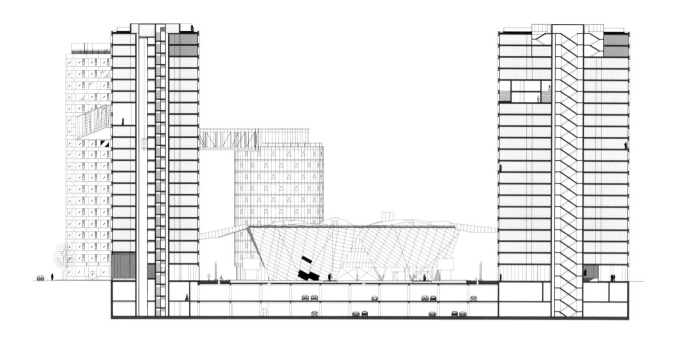

7. A sketch showing kitchen, and dining and living areas.
8, 9. Floor plans of typical units.
10. Movable partitions help create a flow between the unit's private and public spaces.

Red Apple, Rotterdam, Netherlands
Design: KCAP Architects & Planners, 2008

The Red Apple is the sixth tallest building in Rotterdam and includes 231 residential units, office space and retail. Its diverse range of functions is housed in 38 floors with an area of 35,000 m² (376,736 sq. ft.).

The site offers views onto the Maas River and the city's Old Port. Moreover, Red Apple features retail stores, cafés, restaurants, and business spaces, essentially molding many urban features into a single structure. Located on Wijnhaven Island, the designers intended the project to form a dynamic link between the city center and the river. Interestingly enough, Red Apple sits at a visually prominent point flanked by water on three sides. As intended, the building is a combination of various architectural masses, featuring the existing block structure with a height of 21 m (69 ft.), which includes some of the existing office spaces. The weaving of the existing block and the new is part of the envisioned dynamic transformation model. Moreover, the southwest corner of the lot is occupied by a slender tower 124 m (407 ft.) tall. To create a captivating environment, a spacious, glazed ground floor entrance lobby was included. The floors above the lobby contain live-work spaces, while the upper levels feature more conventional apartments of various sizes.

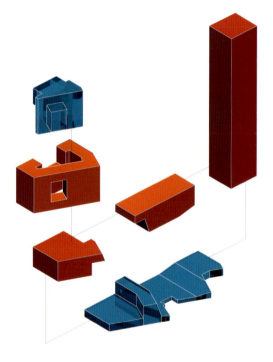

In terms of geometry, the converging lines of Wijnhaven Island meet at The Red Apple, outlining a five-sided volume, part of which cantilevers beyond the substructure. Within this block, a range of different-sized apartments surrounds a central atrium. This provides the occupants with a spatial orientation and familiarize them with the internal circulation routes. In addition, the architects decided to employ large apertures in the façade, allowing the atrium to benefit from great views of the city. The outstanding panoramic views demanded prominent use of glass across both the tower and cantilevered block. Floor-to-ceiling solar glass between red bands of anodized aluminum characterizes the façade and accentuates the building in the skyline from afar.

The tower's exterior features red vertical stripes that decrease in thickness towards the top to enhance its slender appearance. On the other hand, the cantilevered block includes horizontal red bands, which define the layered design of building. The red bands are made of anodized aluminum panels. In the tower, the bands adapt in width to the increasing mass towards ground level.

The Red Apple combines several land uses to fit nicely in a challenging urban context and create a welcome addition to the skyline of Rotterdam.

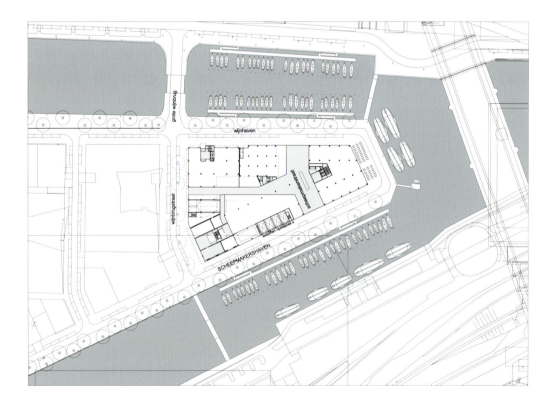

1. A diagrammatic representation of the Red Apple's various functions that include stores, cafés, restaurants and business spaces.
2. Red Apple is located at a visually prominent point in Rotterdam, flanked by water on three sides, as demonstrated in the site plan.
3. The exterior of the Red Apple features vertical stripes that decrease in thickness towards the top to enhance its slender appearance.
4. A view from the penthouse onto the Maas River and the city's Old Port.

5. The glazed walls of the living room offer spectacular views of the exterior.
6, 7. Typical floor plans of the tower.
8. A triangular floor plan of one of the Red Apple's lower levels.
9. A view of the living room from the kitchen in the penthouse.

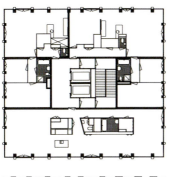

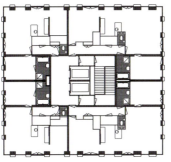

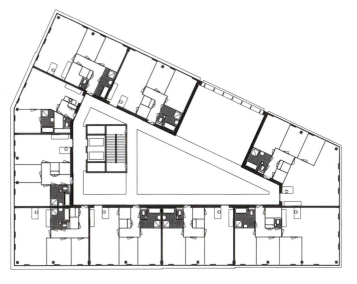

Sonnenhof, Jena, Germany
Design: J. Mayer H und Partner, Architekten, 2013

Located in the historical city center of the city of Jena, the Sonnenhof, a landmark mixed-use building, includes four eight-storey independent structures. Half of the site's area is occupied by four buildings with a total floor area of 10,000 m² (107,639 sq. ft.). The remaining half of the site is utilized as a public space. The buildings, sitting on the edges of the lot, frame a small inner court-yard with remnants of medieval structures. This isolated courtyard, along with the space surrounding it, permits a free flow of pedestrian traffic. Pathways between the buildings connect them to the surrounding areas, making the project an important urban junction. As for the program, mixed-use functions are included to ensure that the complex contribute to the city's center vibrancy.

The façades are made-up of polygonal forms and each of the four buildings is a permutation of regular and irregular polygons clad in a white material. The polygonal shapes are made of the same material as the rest of the envelop but they are tinted black. All of the windows are contained within the black polygons, and are oriented in parallel rows to the ground. The designers continued the polygonal language along the floors of the public space as well.

In addition, the green spaces, which exist throughout, extend the general theme of the project by including other polygonal features. When designing the public spaces, one of the goals was to enhance these areas by including flowerbeds, wedged ventilation openings, irregular seating, and playful lighting. Essentially, the modification of trivial components, such as those noted above, transforms these spaces into attractive leisure areas.

The Sonnenhof is a welcome addition to Jena's historic urban fabric which also created welcoming spaces for the residents and the public.

1. The Sonnenhof project is located in the historical center of the city of Jena.
2, 3. Floor plans. The buildings, set on the edges of the lot, frame a small inner courtyard.

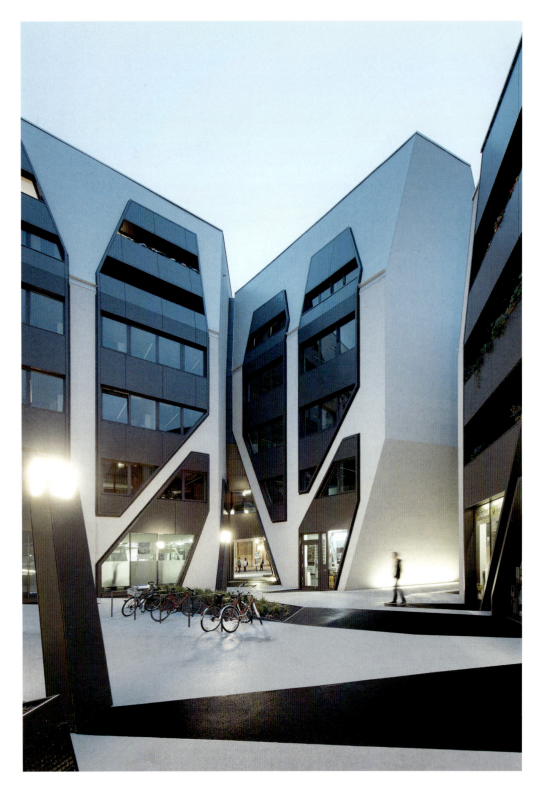

4. Pathways between the buildings connect them to the surrounding areas, making the project an important urban junction.

5. Mixed-use functions have been included in the program to ensure contribution to the city center's vibrancy.

6. The façades are made up of polygonal forms, and each of the four buildings is a permutation of regular and irregular polygons clad in a white material.

Überseequartier SPV 1–4, Hamburg, Germany

Design: Erick van Egeraat, 2011

The mixed-use SPV 1–4 buildings are part of the Überseequartier HafenCity waterfront redevelopment plan in Hamburg, Germany. Completed in 2011, the project has a floor area of 37,000 m² (398,264 sq. ft.) and it is includes housing, retail and office spaces.

As part of the master plan, SPV 1–4 is intended to be a significant focal point in the sector's urban context. In this regard, the designers chose to situate the retail spaces and businesses on the ground floor along Übersee boulevard and the offices and rental apartments on upper levels. In addition to being an urban attraction, the project was also intended to provide exclusive spaces for visitors. As a result, the building forms a clear urban block that surrounds an inner courtyard open to the boulevard. This partially enclosed space creates a semi-private courtyard, which provides a quaint retreat for the residents, while remaining accessible to outsiders. SPV 1–4 stands approximately 11 floors tall, and offers 445 parking spaces for its users. A special feature of the development is its chosen architectural language. First, the beautiful gesture employed along the intersecting axis of two of the façades gives the building a unique form. Instead of a conventional, orthogonal intersection of both façades, part of the volume has been removed to provide a spectacular effect. As experienced by an onlooker, the building seems as if is receding away from the street.

When designing the façades using various materials, the architects chose to form a dialogue with the aesthetic of the historic Speicherstadt. In essence, the architectural traits present along the façades of the new building are intended to embody the aesthetics of the redbrick harbor buildings and the white-plaster walls of the inner city. Consequently, the outer façades facing the streets are mainly comprised of natural stone, elegantly mixed with different shades of glass and aluminum. In contrast, all the façades facing the inner courtyard are white and made entirely of glass. Moreover, the vertical shape of SPV 1–4 is emphasized through the many folds. In addition, the enhanced verticality provides the building with a unique character, allowing it to serve as a focal point. An atrium in the southwestern corner of the complex accentuates the access to the office spaces. The design of the office spaces offer flexible use, with floor areas ranging from 400 m² (4,305 sq. ft.) to 4,000 m² (43,055 sq. ft.). On the other hand, the 81 housing units can be accessed from the boulevard via a generous staircase, flanked by cafés and bars.

The SPV 1–4 mixed-use building offers a much needed urban design solution by connecting Hamburg's inner city with the revitalized waterfront.

1. As part of the master plan for the HafenCity waterfront redevelopment, SPV 1–4 is a significant focal point in the sector as demonstrated by this site plan.
2–4. Floor plans. The building forms a clear urban block that surrounds an inner courtyard which opens to the boulevard. This partially enclosed space creates a semi-private courtyard.
5. The architectural gesture employed along the intersecting axes of two of the façades gives the building a unique form as demonstrated by this street view.

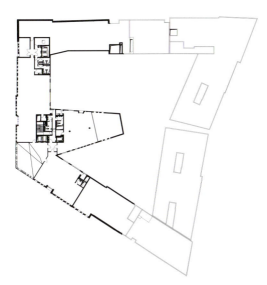

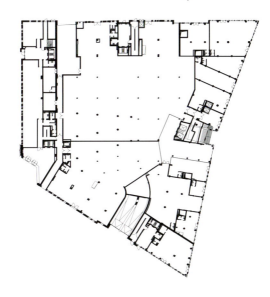

6. Instead of a conventional, orthogonal intersection of both façades, part of the volume has been removed to provide a unique effect where the building seems to be receding from the street.
7. This partially enclosed space creates a semi-private courtyard, which provides a quaint retreat for residents, while remaining accessible to outsiders.
8. The atrium in the southwestern corner of the complex accentuates access to office spaces.

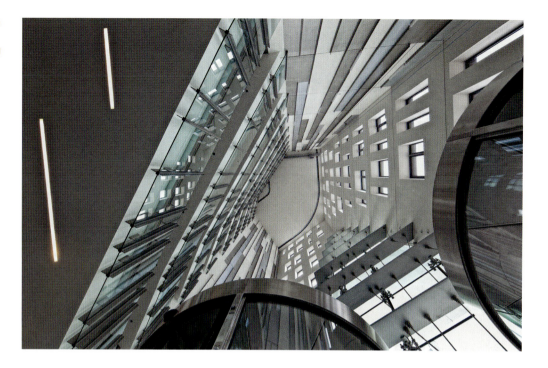

Innovative outdoor areas and meeting spaces

Outdoor places and meeting spaces are essential to a resident's social well-being and physical and mental health. A green landscape also helps preserve an area's bio-diversity, allowing fauna and flora to survive. The importance of these places have become essential given the present shift in cities toward higher density and apartment living. This chapter elaborate on the benefits of these spaces and articulate how they can be integrated in the built environment.

Green areas in or near buildings make communities sustainable in number of ways. For one, they mitigate the urban heat island effect which refers to the fact that the annual air temperature of a city can be warmer than surrounding areas. Urban heat islands also harmfully contribute to peak energy demands in the summer, air conditioning costs, air pollution, greenhouse gas emissions, heat-related illnesses, and lower water quality. Strategically placed trees and shrubbery help alleviate heat peaks, as shaded surfaces are cooler than materials exposed to direct sunlight.

Green areas can also contribute to the residents' well-being by offering the opportunity to engage in an active lifestyle, which helps tackle issues from obesity to mental health. Open public spaces can also counter the effects of crowding to ensure that occupants do not feel confined in their small apartments. In high-density developments it is often difficult to have continuity of open spaces, but is achievable if green corridors link urban natural patches to big parks. The use of indigenous plants in landscape design will help local flora and fauna survive.

The first decision in planning open spaces involves the amount of area that will be devoted to them in the building. Having public space does not imply that it all must be consolidated in a single spot. Often, it is better to distribute them on different levels and in multiple areas to create a variety of smaller, human-scaled places. Proper scale can be ensured through the use of height-to-width ratios. A ratio of 1:3 to 1:5 for common space within a medium to high-density development would be appropriate. Some municipalities also mandate that each dwelling unit will have individual outdoor space in the form of balcony or ground floor yard.

A sense of community is established by having meeting places which encourage interaction among residents. Having such spaces is critical component of community building that lets people share facilities that they would not be able to afford on their own. Open spaces need to be planned in accordance with residents' variable lifestyles and life stages. A divide between areas for intimate versus lively activity should be physically represented in those spaces. Just as spaces can be designed to suit activities, they might also be configured for a specific user group. Infant play spaces require areas for adults to supervise and relax. School-age children require facilities to host a range of activities, and the distribution of open space for this function will vary depending on each building's actual demographic profile.

Within a building, the transition between private and public open spaces might be difficult to define. Yet, establishing this distinction will prevent intrusions on private property and preserve both communal and individual identities. Different levels of private space can exist based on their physical distribution. On-grade space either front, back and side yards help form pleasing environment and even foster better relationships between neighbours. Above-grade space, like balconies and roof terraces permit a greater level of privacy and for some can even offer complete seclusion.

When green areas on or above ground community gardens are provided, they can be private, shared or both. Shared garden plots should have a water supply system and a storage area for tools. Rooftop gardens can be considered when on-grade ground space is otherwise occupied.

It is clear that the planning and provision of open spaces in and around apartment buildings require much care and thought. Private outdoor space, whether in the form of front or back yards, patios, decks, balconies or roof terraces, must be provided along with public outdoor space, which can be implemented in a variety of spatial patterns. Additionally, the design of the landscape itself, including man-made features and vegetation, should be functional and aesthetically appealing to create an inviting environment.

60 Richmond Cooperative Housing, Toronto, Ontario, Canada

Design: Teeple Architects, 2010

60 Richmond Cooperative Housing is an eleven-storey tall apartment building where creating places for social interaction was one of the goals. The building's residential and leisure spaces have a floor area of 9,250 m² (99,565 sq. ft.).

The structure houses 85 units and is a result of collaboration between a local city councilor, the hospitality workers' union UNITE HERE and Toronto Community Housing. The occupants, many of whom work in the restaurant and hospitality industries, have been relocated to the project as part of the revitalization of the Regent Park social housing initiative.

The program sought to incorporate outdoor spaces for local food production. As a result, the architects designed what is known as an urban permaculture. For example, the resident-owned and operated restaurants, as well as training kitchen on the ground floor, supplied by produce grown on the sixth floor terrace. By extension, this notion of urban permaculture is multi-faceted and affects more than one level of functions. The garden is irrigated by storm water runoff from the roof. In addition, the organic waste produced by the restaurant and training kitchen is collected and used as compost to nourish the roof garden making the building self-sufficient.

When referring to its design, unlike the myriad of condominiums visible in downtown Toronto, 60 Richmond was conceived as a solid mass that was carved-into to create openings and terraces at various levels. The deconstruction of its mass results in open spaces stepping out and back from the street level. More importantly, the visually appealing and fluent gestures employed by the architects is integral in achieving certain goals. These include but are not limited to drawing light into the building's interior. In addition, the garden terraces help cool and cleanse the air, which ultimately limits the urban heat island effect.

The client's requirement for low maintenance costs also inspired many of the design and sustainable innovations. Durable materials were combined with energy saving strategies such as insulating fiber cement panel cladding, high performance windows, a sophisticated mechanical system, as well as drain water heat recovery from the common laundry facilities.

With the 60 Richmond Cooperative Housing project, Teeple Architects created an innovative, visually striking, apartment building, which is able to use spatial constraints to increase the usable space of the building.

1. 60 Richmond Cooperative Housing is an 11-storey apartment building in the heart of Toronto that offers opportunities for social interaction among residents.
2. 60 Richmond was conceived as a solid mass that was carved-into to create openings and terraces at various levels.

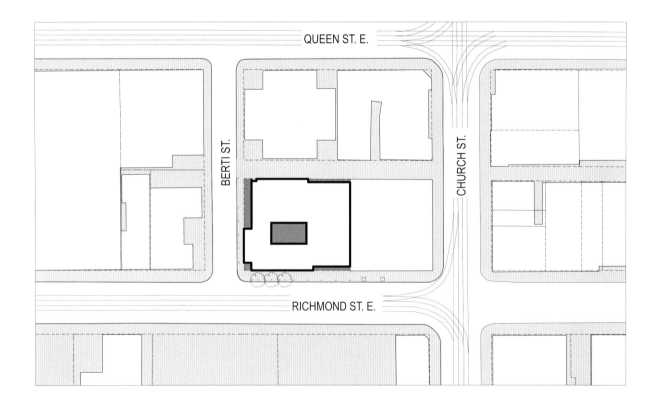

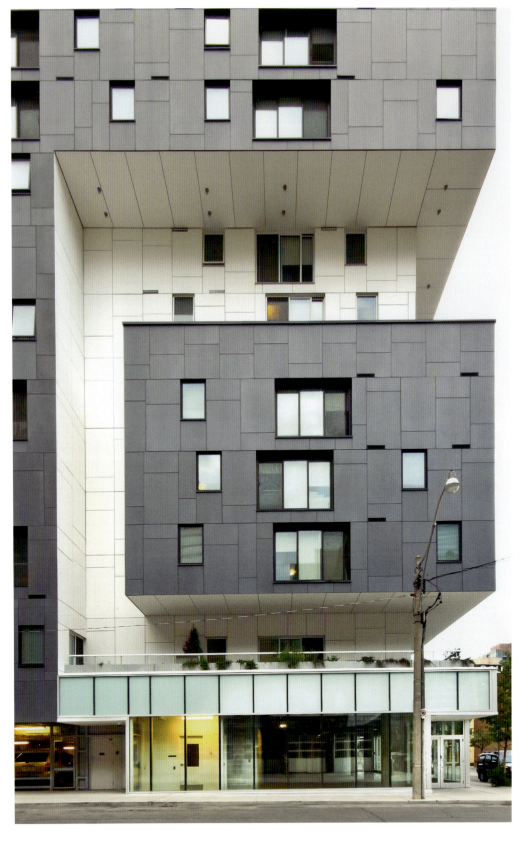

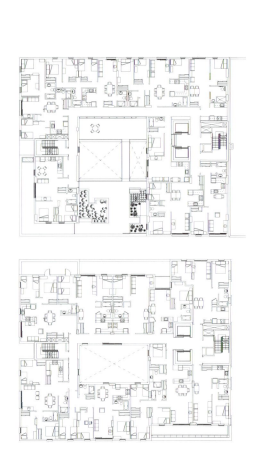

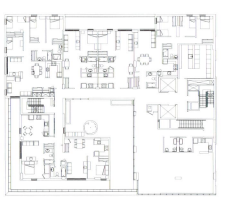

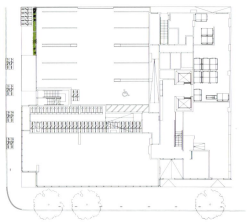

3. The deconstruction of 60 Richmond's mass results in open spaces stepping out and back from the street level.

4–7. Floor plans. The program of 60 Richmond sought to incorporate outdoor spaces for local food production in what is known as an urban permaculture. For example, the resident-owned and operated restaurants, as well as training kitchen on the ground floor, use produce grown on the sixth-floor terrace.

8. A section showing the openings and terraces.

9. A view from a unit's living room.

10. A view of the open areas of the building that help draw light into the interior as well as increase cross ventilation.

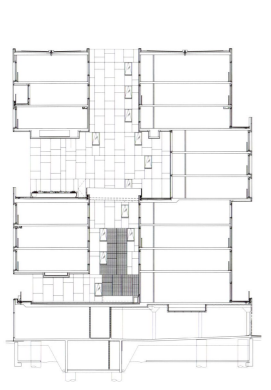

625 Rhode Island Avenue, Washington, D.C., USA

Design: Suzane Reatig Architecture, 2012

The 625 Rhode Island Avenue project responds to one of the many growing needs of contemporary apartment building architecture: high-density living. It features 16 units and a floor area of 2,985 m² (32,125 sq. ft.) on four levels. Located in close proximity to a metro stop, one of its sides faces the street and the other one is bounded by a public alley.

The project's main goals were to provide much needed housing for families in the heart of the city and leave sufficient public spaces. To reserve enough space for public use while maximizing the number of dwelling units, the architect determined that increasing density would make most sense which in addition to zoning bylaws lead to the chosen number of units and height.

In addition, the four-storey LEED-certified building features a green roof, a courtyard and a linear garden. The garden follows the contour of the lot, and occupies space between the apartment building and the neighboring public alleyway. Similarly, the semi-private courtyard space is encased by the building itself and by a public alleyway. This layout serves a two-fold purpose: it provides the residents with privacy, and also offers space to visitors who would like to enjoy it occasionally.

As a response to the site's topography, the building gently steps up in scale from the lower two- and three-storey residences to the taller, denser intersection of 7th Street and Rhode Island Avenue. More importantly, the garden creates a buffer zone for the west facing housing units. By the same token, this linear garden creates another open public space along the public alley, rendering it safe and pleasant. The interior courtyard, garden, and green roof effectively create opportunities for the occupants to socialize.

In terms of design constraints, the long and narrow site, along with small budget, were seen as an opportunity for innovation. The bold exterior colors employed along the façades give the building a unique identity, and engage the curiosity of passers-by. In stark contrast with the vivid character of the exterior, its interior is rather serene. The multitude of exposures and large operable windows showcased by the architect provide cross ventilation and plenty of sunlight. The designers also included another interesting »green« feature to this project via the balconies. Essentially, deep balconies provide for passive exterior shading, and the high-pressure laminate rain screen system ensures that the building envelope can »breathe« without letting moisture to penetrate in.

1. Located in close proximity to a metro stop, one side of 625 Rhode Island Avenue faces the street (shown in this image) and the other is bounded by a public alley.
2, 3. Floor plans. The layout of the building serves a two-fold purpose: it provides the residents with privacy, and its semi-private courtyard offers space for the enjoyment of occasional visitors.
4. The bold exterior colors employed along the façades give the building a unique identity, and engage the curiosity of passers-by.

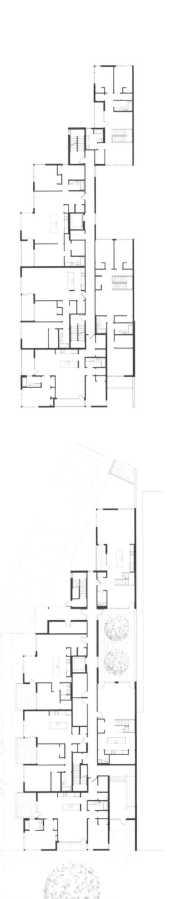

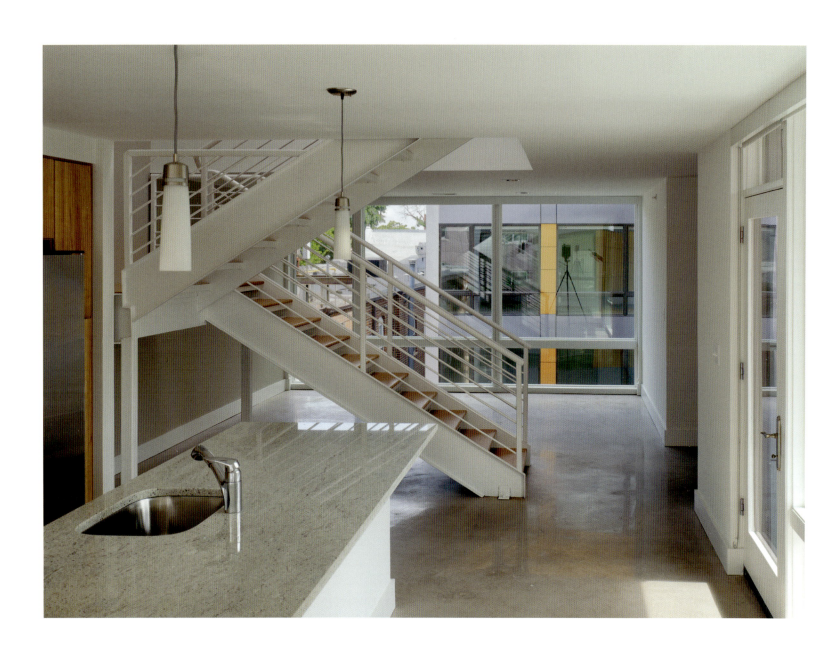

5. The multitude of exposures and large operable windows showcased by the architect provide cross ventilation and plenty of sunlight.
6. The deep balconies provide for passive exterior shading, and the high-pressure laminate rain screen system ensures that the building envelope can »breathe« without allowing moisture to penetrate.
7. A view from a unit into the courtyard.

High Park, San Pedro Garza García, Mexico
Design: rojkind arquitectos Michel Rojkind, 2014

The High Park apartment building includes 32 units with a floor area of 33,000 m² (355,209 sq. ft.) that stands ten storeys tall, and houses 3 penthouse units on its uppermost level.

Influenced by its close proximity to the majestic Sierra Madre Oriental Range, the designers' conceived this project to maximize views and help mitigate the region's extreme climactic conditions by having cross ventilation. As a result, the stale air in the building is constantly being replaced by fresh air. In addition, the cross ventilation aids in reducing the building's temperature without using mechanical means. The designers also chose to employ a thick envelop which protects the interior from the sun.

When designing High Park, the architects faced the challenge of integrating the building into the pedestrian realm as a way of »giving back« to the community. The chosen solution was to gradually recess the building and step it back to create an outdoor shaded space that can be enjoyed by all. Gerardo Salinas, one of the principal architects, explains that often times, apartment building architecture does not allow for the creation of public spaces. Rather, the entire site is developed and devised to optimize the square footage available for economic gain. To counter this notion, the designers took special care and reserved public spaces to be used by all.

The apartment building's staggered level arrangement does not only enhance the project's aesthetic appeal, it is also meant to counterbalance the effect of the strong sun. As a result, the floor plates shift in relation to one another creating a play of light and shadow, and the use of stone by a local craftsman on the façade allows the building to stay cooler as the sun moves across the horizon.

Multiple strict setback restrictions of the site resulted in private outdoor terraces for each apartment to enjoy. These outdoor spaces also capitalize on the panoramic views of the nearby Majestic Sierra Madre Oriental Range and adjacent mountains. Moreover, High Park consists of ten levels above ground, and three and a half levels of underground parking. The space is subdivided; the first two levels are reserved for commercial use, and the remaining eight are dedicated to luxury apartments. The eight residential levels also include amenities such as pool, gym and spa. Each apartment has a different area and configuration ranging from 250 m² (2691 sq. ft.) to 650 m² (6997 sq. ft.).

Essentially, the High Park development features meticulous design and green features which respond to its location. Rojkind arquitectos' designed a building, which does not only showcase a structure, but reserves public spaces for residents and visitors to enjoy.

1. Site plan (when designing High Park, the architects integrated the building into the pedestrian realm. As a result, the building steps back to create an outdoor shaded space that can be enjoyed by all).
2. The staggered level arrangement of the High Park apartment building not only enhances the project's aesthetic appeal, but it is also meant to counterbalance the effect of the strong sun.
3. The floors of High Park are subdivided; the first two levels are reserved for commercial use, and the remaining eight are dedicated to apartments as demonstrated in this section.

pp. 76, 77
4–7. Floor plans. The staggering of the floors in High Park and the integration of residential and commercial land uses coupled with the creation of a public space contributed to the success of this project.
8. The site of High Park was designed to optimize the area and leave public spaces for use by the public and the residents as demonstrated in this image.
9. The multiple strict setback restrictions of the site resulted in private outdoor terraces for each apartment as demonstrated in this night view.

AERIAL VIEW

Santa Magdalena

25° 38' 48.70" N
100° 21' 40.80" O

9th Side Street

9th Street

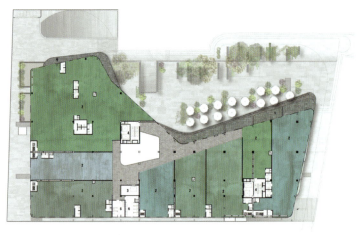

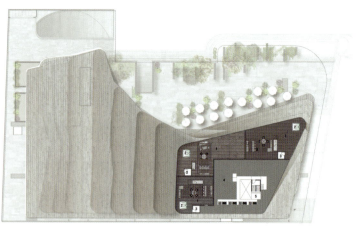

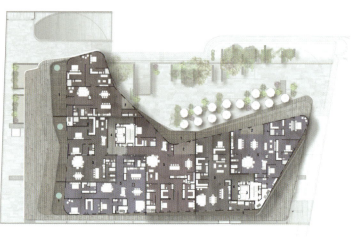

Reflections, Keppel Bay, Singapore
Design: Studio Daniel Libeskind, 2011

With a floor area of 185,806 m² (2,000,000 sq. ft.), this innovative complex is comprised of six high-rise towers ranging from twenty-four to forty-one storeys and eleven low-rise villa apartment blocks of six to eight floors and a total of 1,129 units. When designing Reflections, the architect felt the need to create a focal point. Consequently, the high-rise undulating towers are quite captivating from afar. These sleek curving forms of alternating heights create graceful openings and gaps between the structures allowing all to have commanding views of the waterfront, the golf course and Mount Faber in the distance.

When the development is looked at in greater detail, one notices that it is composed of two distinct housing typologies; the first being the lower villas along the waterfront and the second the towers, which overlook them from behind. As intended by the architects, the variation of forms and the succinct balance between the short and the tall structures creates an overall open and light ambiance.

In addition, the noticeable ambiguity in the building forms creates a unique experience for the residents since each floor is not aligned with the one above, below it, or in a building adjacent to it. As a result, no two apartment units are experienced in the same fashion because each of them offers a different perspective. This changing viewpoint also provides an exclusive and dynamic feel to each unit since it enhances a sense of individuality. In a project of such large magnitude and great density, it is often difficult to allow each unit to be distinct. However, through this ambiguous and off-axis design, Studio Daniel Libeskind managed to conceive a community of apartment buildings in which individuality and difference for each residence is not sacrificed. The varying heights of the structures also allow for footbridges to link them. The architect also placed many open spaces across all levels to encourage social encounters between residents. At a central point within the development, there are many amenities including a gym, lobby and outdoor swimming pool for residents to enjoy.

As a result of its innovative and contemporary design, Reflections was awarded the BCA Green Mark Gold Award from Singapore's building and construction authority.

1. Site plan. Located at Keppel Bay, Singapore, Reflections comprise of six high-rise towers ranging from twenty-four to forty-one storeys and eleven low-rise villa apartment blocks of six to eight floors and a total of 1,129 units.
2. The sleek curving forms of the towers and their alternating heights create graceful openings and gaps between the structures allowing all to have commanding views of the waterfront, the golf course and Mount Faber in the distance.
3, 4. Floor plans (in Reflections no two apartment units have the same view because each of them offers a different perspective. This changing viewpoint also provides an exclusive and dynamic feel to each unit since it enhances a sense of individuality).

pp. 78, 79
5. The development includes many amenities such as a gym and outdoor swimming pool for residents to enjoy as demonstrated in this view.
6, 7. Interior views of a two-storey unit. The open plan concept creates a flow of spaces between the levels and the different rooms.

SITE PLAN
1:1000

TOWER 2B
22ND STOREY PLAN (REFUGE FLOOR)

BLK A & F
2ND & 4TH STOREY PLAN

Solid 11, Amsterdam, Netherlands

Design: Tony Fretton Architects, 2011

A notable example of sustainable design is the Solid 11 apartment building in Amsterdam. This novel structure contains 33 units, in an 8,000 m² (86,111 sq. ft.) of mixed-use space.

The design of this seven-storey building was based on two important criteria: longevity and open areas within the structure. To satisfy the longevity criterion, the architects designed the project with a 200-year lifespan in mind. This durable and extended lifespan were inspired by the Dutch housing association Stadgenoot. For the same reasons, the apartment building's name »Solid 11« is derived from Stadgenoot's definition of a solid: a highly durable and sustainable typology.

As an inspiration for this design, the architects sought to replicate certain characteristics omnipresent in Amsterdam's old squats. Essentially, these layouts resemble loft buildings, which include narrow floor plates, high floor-to-ceiling heights, ample daylight and considerable structural capacity. There are also two wings on either side of a central courtyard. The architects managed to persuade the client to allow them to employ a central courtyard that was extended to the ground. Their aim in doing so was to create a public space that might attract social activities to the units.

As a method of respecting the notion of »solid« in this development, the architects employed palazzo-esque features to the façades. Therefore, the façades of the building's twin structures are treated as a continuous row of piers. The base upon which they reside is made of porphyry, and the structure extends upwards in self-supporting brick. To accentuate the height of the loft-style spaces, glazed doors are set between them and separated in turn by brick-faced spandrel panels. Along the long, south-facing façade, the designers introduced projecting balconies, while the canal side is addressed with a continuous first-floor terrace. In contrast to both these façades, the architects chose to exhibit classical features along the street façade. Moreover, the stone base rises 1 m (3.3 ft.) above street level and acquire a stringcourse, providing it with a much-increased compositional weight, while the building's top two storeys are fashioned into form of a crown.

Interestingly enough, the red-brown brick on the outer façades transitions to a light-reflective blond variety along the courtyard elevations. External galleries are carried along the full extent of these façades, their floors in glass block and their balustrades in glass. The external galleries make for remarkable architectural details. The steel beams on which they are supported cantilever not from the explicitly load-bearing brick piers that the building's tectonic logic suggests they should be, but rather from the intervening spandrel panels. Luckily, these are load-bearing and have been recessed and covered in vertically coursed brickwork. Glass-bottomed bridges at either end of the galleries establish a complete circuit at each level. In addition, the central courtyard features a six-storey glass acoustic screen.

As a result of these attributes, this building is made even more attractive by its flexible nature. It is presented to the public as a shell in which tenants are offered flexibility to decide on size, configuration and use of space.

1. Solid 11 is embedded in an established urban area. In fact, as an inspiration for this design, the architects sought to replicate certain characteristics omnipresent in Amsterdam's old districts.
2–5. Floor plans. The layout of the floors in Solid 11 resembles loft buildings, which include narrow floor plates, high floor-to-ceiling heights, ample daylight and considerable structural capacity.

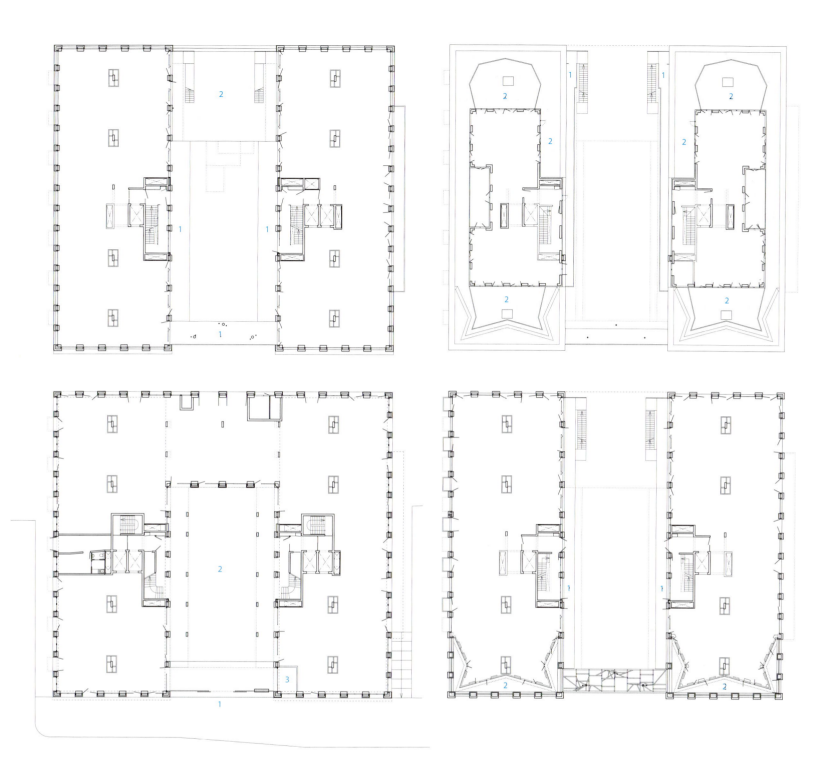

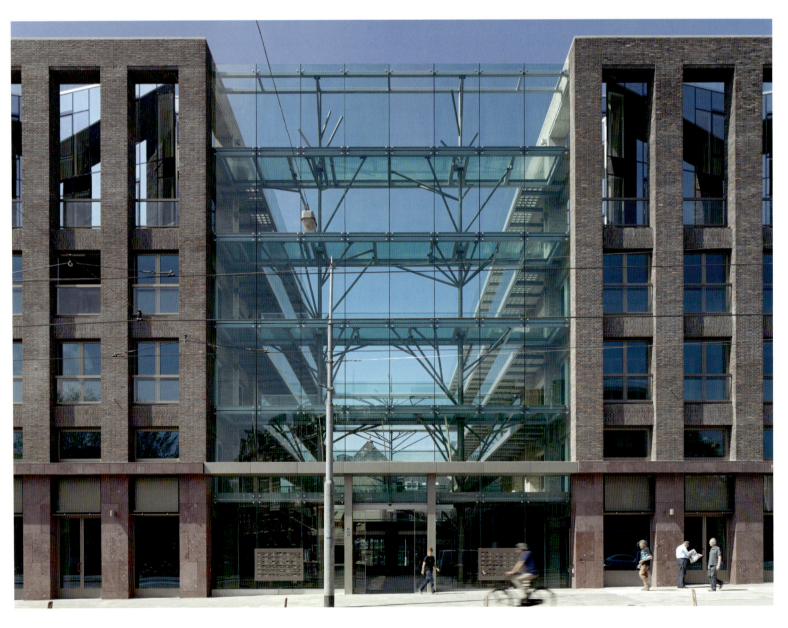

6. The architects employed palazzo-esque features to the façades treating them as a continuous row of piers.
7. The building is made up of two wings on either side of a central courtyard that offers a public space for social activities.

Converting old structures to contemporary residential use

Reusing old buildings can benefit the environment and the locations in which they are constructed. The process is known to reduce energy consumption and prevent urban sprawl. Culturally, conservation helps foster a local identity, ties the past to the future and contributes to heritage preservation. This chapter explores the conversion of existing structures to apartment buildings.

Building conversion consists of finding a new purpose for old structures whose current uses are no longer viable. For example, multi-storey industrial buildings that have closed down may be suitable for conversion. The transformation in methods of industrial production from multi-storey to a single level and the preference to relocate modern plants near highways vacated factories in the heart of cities. With the rise in the value of urban living, investments in converting such buildings become economically viable, leading to growing interest in such projects.

Demographic changes over time offer another opportunity for initiators of conversion projects. As traditional nuclear families no longer constitute the majority among households in western nations, singles, single-parent families and the elderly are more inclined to look for smaller, lower cost dwellings built in higher density settings. Living next to existing amenities and not relying entirely on private cars becomes another attraction.

Another potential benefit of converted buildings is their effect on the surrounding area. Well-designed project can help revitalize a neighborhood. By attracting more residents, new developments can broaden an area's tax base by attracting new business. By providing a variety of unit types, a wide range of households can reside in the same neighborhood to create a healthy sociodemographic mix.

When zoning permits, these projects also provides an opportunity for mixed-use projects to combine residential, retail and community functions within the same structure that further contributes to vibrant city life. Depends on location, converted structures also tend to produce smaller-sized affordable units which appeals to certain households.

Despite the seemingly many advantages of converted projects, the problems surrounding them lead to building challenges. When an entire area or a single building remains vacant, there is usually a good reason for it. For example, when the building is the former location of a manufacturing plant or storage facility, poisonous materials have found their way into the floors, and may pose a risk. The structure, therefore, needs to be tested and decisions as to the method of the clean-up made.

The size, shape and location of the building may also make the project more challenging to design and costly to build. To efficiently design such projects, their shape may lead to substantial waste that can cast doubts on their economic viability. Close attention also must be paid to parking there if too many additional cars need to be accommodated.

Several views have been introduced to guide the architectural preservation of old buildings. The conservationist view encourages strict preservation. A functionalist view, on the other hand, mediates heritage conflicts that arise between economic and cultural values. The sense of place perspective combines the two preceding principles of preservation. Instead of focusing on specific buildings, this view captures the uniqueness of the location as a whole.

Heritage preservation strategies for a building's conversion cannot be applied uniformly. Familiarity with the original date of construction will lead to knowledge about a building's style and construction techniques. A study of the building's exterior features can offer advice as to a range and type of components that should be respected as the rehabilitation begins. The elements to be studied are cladding materials, decorative wood or brickwork, and window and door types.

The design of the dwelling can proceed in several stages. First the socio-demographic composition of potential buyers needs to be determined, followed by decision on the number of units and their price range. Design flexibility can be achieved by creating open spaces with predetermined wet walls. The process can become one of adapting a generic volume to the buyer's particular spatial and economic specifications. The clients may select kitchens and bathrooms from a menu of offerings and then decided on their location in the purchased spaces. The result can be a range of affordable dwelling units which meet the space needs and means of the buyer.

Heritage conservation and sustainable development work hand in hand since they address similar concerns. While current planning policies aim to address contemporary social issues, it is important to remember that old structures on their heritage value need not to be forgotten.

71 Apartments, Sète, France
Design: Colboc Franzen & Associés, 2011

The 71 Apartments development in Sète, France was built on an abandoned strip of land on the northern side of the town near the Mediterranean Sea. The development includes three towers, two that stand eight storeys tall, while the third rises to six storeys.

The project is the first stage in an ambitious urban renewal that aims to convert huge swathes of abandoned docklands into a business and residential use. Furthermore, the lot is located in close proximity to the port on its huge industrial facilities. The project consists of three apartment blocks that include 16 social-housing units, 55 private two- and three-room apartments, as well as shops and a parking space. The architects decided to place the private apartments in the two eight-storey towers, while the smaller six-storey block house the social housing portraying the site planning process as placing an object in the midst of an island.

When contemplating the design, the designers questioned how to evoke the site's past and at the same time, through architecture, forge a modern identity for this entrance point to the town of Sète and its emerging neighborhoods. In addition, they were concerned with the building's response to the vast scale of the port, with the sea as the horizon, while also maintaining the old town's way of living.

As a common link between the three independent structures, the architects established a podium, which extends between them, concealing a large parking area beneath a row of shops. In terms of placement, the shortest six-storey block is positioned at the center of the lot to provide a smooth transition between the urban renewal and existing buildings around it. Consequently, the two tallest blocks are placed along the outskirts, to freely display their autonomy. The eight-storey structure, which sits along the street corner, represents the entrance from the old town, while also providing a view onto the port facilities and future development of the empty docklands. The rear structure was placed on parking spaces and includes gardens.

The designers also decided to include features of Mediterranean architecture as well. As a result, the buildings allow for a lifestyle adapted for the local climate by providing spaces for outdoor living sheltered from heat and balconies that run along every façade. These outdoor protrusions allow residents to enjoy these exterior spaces as they please. Across all three buildings, the architects employed a galvanized steel screen as a main material. More specifically, curved, galvanized steel grids shelter the façades and outdoor balconies. This eloquent feature protects the units and their outdoor quarters from intense heat, while also provide each unit with privacy. Furthermore, at times the buildings appear as large steel objects, which remind the public of the area's maritime heritage.

The 71 Apartments development demonstrates that contemporary architecture can make a contribution to urban renewal while at the same time fitting well with the context.

1. The 71 Apartments development was built on a strip of land on the northern side of the town of Sète, France near the Mediterranean Sea.
2. The site of the 71 Apartments development is located in close proximity to the port and its huge industrial facilities and was the first stage in an ambitious urban renewal project.
3, 4. Floor plans. The project consists of three apartment blocks that include social-housing units, private two- and three-room apartments, as well as shops and a parking space.

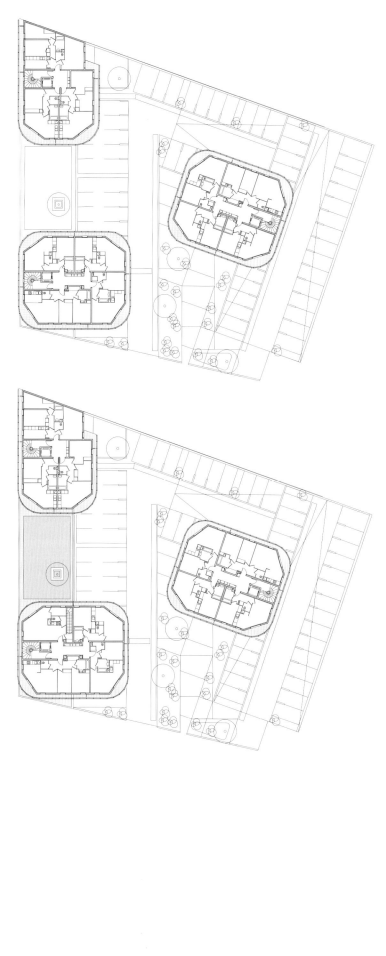

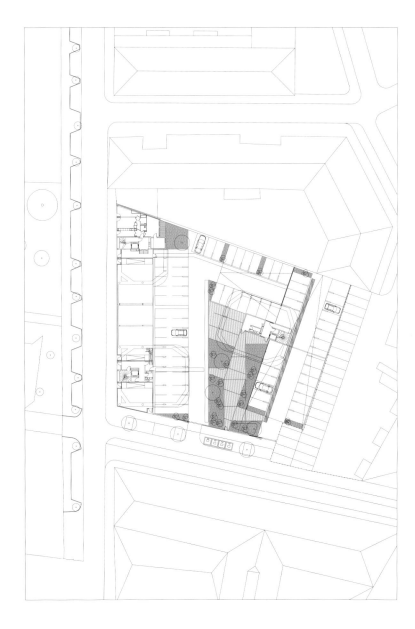

5. A view from one of the buildings onto the port area.

6. The design allows spaces for outdoor living sheltered from heat and balconies that run along every façade by using galvanized steel grids.

7. The designers evoke the site's past through architecture and forge a modern identity for this entrance point to the town of Sète.

Siloetten, Løgten, Denmark
Design: C.F. Møller Architects, 2010

The Siloetten building is part of an urban renewal development that stands eleven storeys tall, with a floor area of 3,100 m² (33,368 sq. ft.) and includes 21 high-quality apartments. The project utilizes existing infrastructure in an innovative and practical way.

A method called spolia was used in the conversion of the derelict spaces. The method entails use of fragments or remnants of an existing structure and its site as building blocks for the new development. As a result, the Siloetten was transformed from a former silo complex into a high-quality building composed of individual and unique stacked villas.

The renewal of this type of silo is significant in Denmark since these abandoned structures dominate the countryside's skyline. Therefore, converting them into rural high-rise buildings was an effective method of heritage preservation. The development is quite unique in the sense that the units are not configured as they would be in a typical apartment block. Instead, they are a mix of single-storey flats and two-storeys units also known as maisonettes.

The Siloetten integrated the original structure of the silo complex to give it new, purposeful functions. The actual silo contained staircases and lifts, and provided the base for project's common roof terrace. Around this existing structure, the architects included an eye-catching steel structure, on which the apartments rest. Similar to lego bricks, the apartments protrude from the structure and interact in intriguing ways with the external light. Moreover, this extraordinary structure includes protrusions and displacements, which allow each of the 21 apartments to benefit from generous outdoor spaces, views of the Aarhus Bay and the city.

To provide the building with other functions besides housing, the architects incorporated a mixed-use space at the foot of the former silo. As a result, a new »village-center« was created, offering a public space surrounded by shops, supermarkets, terraced housing, and a green park dedicated to the residents. In converting the former structure, the architects ensured that the nature of the development remains unique. Since it is conversion, no other building in the area can be built to the same height, therefore allowing Siloetten to remain a tall freestanding landmark.

1. Siloetten was a transformation project of a former silo complex into a high-quality building composed of individual and stacked units.
2. A diagram showing the variety of unit types that were included in the project and their interlocking arrangement. Similar to Lego bricks, the apartments protrude from the structure in intriguing ways.
3. Photo of the original silo structure that was used as the base for the new development.
4. The actual silo contained staircases and lifts. Around this existing structure, the architects built a new steel structure for the apartments.

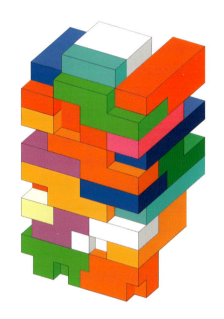

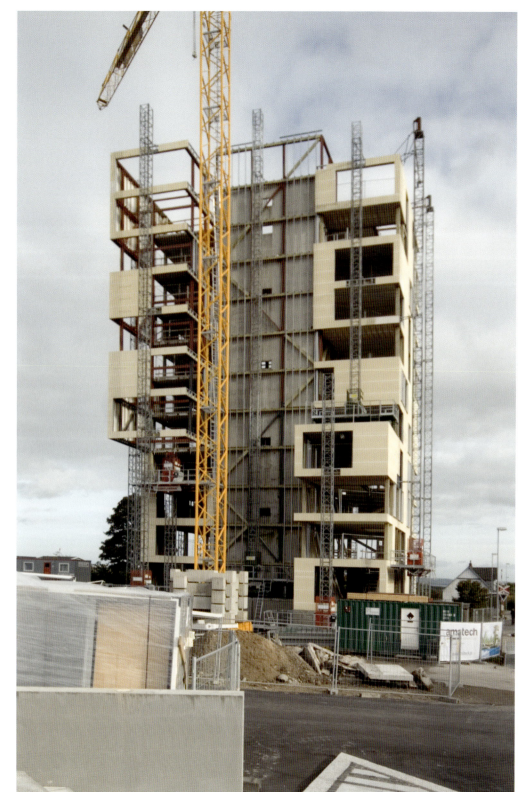

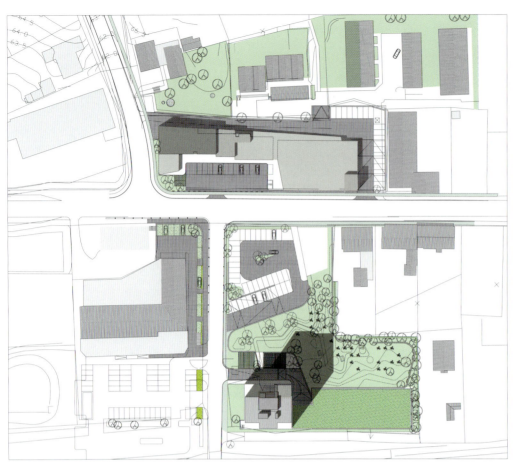

5. A site plan showing the converted building in its context.

6. As a result of the transformation, a new »village-center« was created, offering a public space surrounded by shops, supermarkets, terraced housing, and a green park dedicated to the residents.

7–9. Floor plans. The designers created a variety of unit types to appeal to a wider range of families.

10. The final appearance of Siloetten exterior. The project is a prime example of the potential of conversion projects of this type.

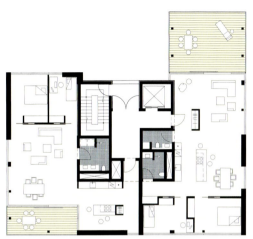

A-House, Copenhagen, Denmark
Design: Holgaard Architects, 2010

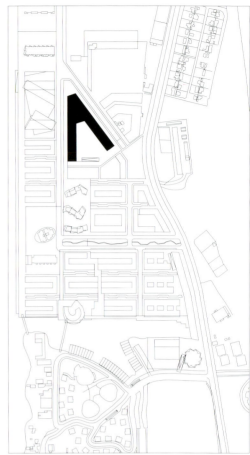

The A-House apartment block is a recent building transformation in Copenhagen that utilizes the remnants of a former industrial structure which dates back to the 1960s. This seven-storey development has a floor area of 23,000 m² (247,569 sq. ft.) and houses 200 units. In addition to residential spaces, this structure offers other mixed-use functions that include commercial areas, furnished apartments, laundry facility and a fitness center. In the roof level, there are seven penthouse units, which are covered by decking and greenery.

The building's industrial history and character inspired the conversion process. Therefore, during the transformation, the architects combined the old industrial building with a new and modern expression without compromising the unique character of the old.

In the interior of A-House, the architects opted for non-conventional solutions. Interestingly, these bold design decisions have resulted in beautiful apartments, made primarily of concrete and surfaces of granite. Although color sometimes injects more life into a building, the gray scale pallet employed, suits the structure's character and historic appeal. The black and white interiors of the units are strikingly beautiful. Moreover, the sharp contrasts are accentuated by the abundance of light, which floods the units via the floor-to-ceiling height windows. As a result, with this transformation the architects also revitalized its exterior.

The building was given a thorough facelift, and the former cladding was completely removed. As a replacement, a new, transparent glass façade was applied along the entire exterior. This elegant glass exterior was then framed in bronze-colored aluminum, giving the building an entirely new appearance and a distinguish character. In addition to the exquisite interior and exterior transformations, the roof-level was also modified. The conversion has led to increased attention towards open, recreational space and in this respect the roof was constructed as a 4,000 m² (43,055 sq. ft.) landscape with hills, pastures and decking.

The A-House apartment block demonstrates that regardless of age, some buildings can undergo a retooling process to extend their life and make them suited to new uses.

1. The A-House apartment block is a recent building transformation in Copenhagen that utilizes the remnants of a former industrial structure which dates back to the 1960s.

2. The A-House is sited in a former industrial area which is undergoing urban transformation.

3. A floor plan of a typical level that demonstrates the approach to the conversion where new stairs were inserted to create walk-up units.

4. The building's exterior was given a thorough facelift, and the former cladding was completely removed. As a replacement, a new transparent glass façade was applied along the entire exterior that was then framed in bronze-colored aluminum.

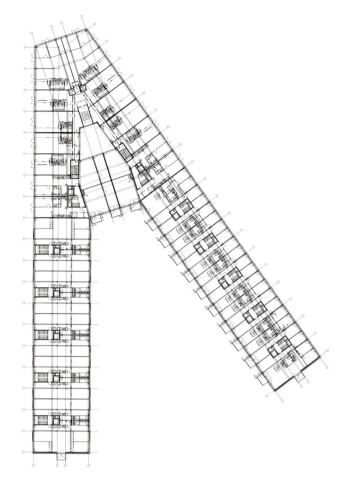

5. View of the kitchen-dining areas.
6. View of the bedroom. In the interiors the sharp contrasts are accentuated by the abundance of light which floods the units via the floor-to-ceiling height windows.

Unique building methods and materials

Construction methods and materials need to be selected carefully since poor choices may adversely affect the architectural performance and appearance of a building. This chapter examines materials and methods that are suitable for apartment buildings.

In general, building materials can be divided to naturally occurring and man-made. Naturally occurring includes organic materials such as wood and minerals. Man-made products are derived from natural resources through physical, mechanical or chemical processing and include cement, plastics and paints. Throughout the design, when considering choice of materials, there are many opportunities to reduce their environmental impact. In a cradle-to-cradle study of materials the main aspects to be considered will be the effect of their production on fossil fuel depletion and emission, transport, toxicity, waste disposal and water extraction.

Resources are considered renewable when they can be naturally replenished and their acquisition remains sustainable, or non-renewable, when they are available on earth in limited and finite amounts. During acquisition, raw materials are mined, quarried, harvested or extracted from natural resources. The process is capable not only of depleting those resources but damaging the surrounding area as will be noted below on some common materials used in the construction of apartment buildings.

Concrete is formed from a mixture of water, sand and gravel solidified together by a binding agent called cement. The acquisition of raw materials for the production of concrete is very energy and resource intensive. It requires extensive mining and quarrying for crushed rock, sand, limestone, clay and coal. It can lead to a number of adverse effects such as deforestation, top soil loss and erosion. To reduce the negative environmental effect of concrete, soil contamination should be minimized through limiting water use in washing equipment, thereby reducing waste water and preventing run-off from the wetting of concrete for curing.

Two of the primary metals used in construction are aluminum and steel. Aluminum is a highly workable, lightweight, durable and strong metal that, depending on its finish, requires little maintenance. Its acquisition involves mining for bauxite ore, a finite resource that comprises roughly eight percent of the earth's crust.

During the manufacturing of aluminum, the smelting process also generates airborne emissions, which are either treated or destroyed. Another drawback of aluminum is the amount of energy that is required for its manufacturing. To reduce the negative environmental effects of aluminum, architectural details should avoid mixed-material assemblies to facilitate recycling. Recovery systems in the building industry should also be established. To lower energy consumption during manufacturing, recycled aluminum can be used in production rather than bauxite ore. Steel is an alloy made of iron and carbon. Like aluminum, it is also strong, durable and workable. Steel, however, corrodes and requires more maintenance and more frequent replacement than aluminum. During the acquisition of raw materials for steel, mining of iron ore is needed, which, when not regulated, may result in mineral depletion and damage to land and wildlife habitat. To increase its sustainability, recycled steel should be used in place of raw materials.

To minimize a building material's adverse effect on the environment, its impact must first be understood and evaluated at every stage of its life cycle. The best materials are those that are referred to as green building materials. Products that use natural local resources or recycled ingredients in place of virgin ones, recycle any waste generated by its processes, have low embodied energy, are biodegradable, have minimal derivation from petrochemicals and are designed for reuse and recyclability are considered the most sustainable. They are also nontoxic, nonhazardous, recyclable or reusable, locally obtained, energy and water efficient, durable as well as environmentally responsible in manufacturing, occupancy and demolition.

In regard to construction methods, prefabrication is celebrated for its accelerated project schedule. Pre-assembled steel elements, key to rapid construction, can be hoisted into place with a crane and bolted together to allow beams and columns to meet at connections points as opposed to welds.

This type of construction draws attention to the importance of designing for a small margin of error. The danger of rehearsing assembly with digital tools is in their unattainable precision. With most of the assembly occurring in the factory, miscalculation or material failures can significantly disturb or interrupt on-site processes.

The future of prefabrication and rapid construction will unfold in tandem with building information modeling (BIM) software. It looks as if in the future more aspects of building construction will be industrialized rather than constructed on site.

Simplon A, Budapest, Hungary

Design: Turányi & Turányi Architects Ltd., 2010

The Simplon A project constitutes the residential portion of a mixed-use development situated in the southwestern part of Budapest. It has quickly become a colorful and vibrant part of the neighborhood's urban landscape.

This innovative apartment building stands out from the existing urban fabric due to both its form and context. As such, the building is rounded and wraps around the main corner of the two large streets it rests against. In fact, this rounded corner makes the main street façades seem unified as one elongated elevation. The fillet edge evokes the architecture of the early modernism; such a rhythm of the façade boxes appears in many modern apartments of the surroundings that were built in the 1960s. T2.a Architects' main design concept was to establish a versatile façade that changes with response to everyday use. These apartments all have large, open façades with well-utilizable covered terraces. The large openings of the façade are shaded by adjustable aluminum louvers; besides the sun protection, the additional role is that they allow the light in; therefore, they serve as an excellent personalized visual filter. Moreover, the color of lamellas is tailored to the color of their particular flat. This way, when the louvers are all shut, the building becomes a box built of LEGO cubes.

The exterior façade of Simplon A employs rather particular materials, the most notable being colored glass. These include bright and unmixed colors like yellow, orange, red, green, dark green, blue turquoise and dark blue. Each color along the façade is attributed to a certain residence. This identifiable color appears once more at the main door of that particular flat. As a result, each residence is marked visually, making the identification of each resident/family's dwelling simple and playful. This residential block is also very easy to access and maneuver through. The flats can be reached through two vertical transportation cores, which are placed in the two breakpoints of the U-shaped building. Open-side corridors connect the elevators and stairs through each flat to promote natural ventilation and lighting on both sides, a tradition in vernacular architecture in Budapest. These open corridors face the miscellaneous and quiet internal garden and the overgrown green-wall. Also, the southern wing of the building is elevated on two »V« shaped legs in order to create a semi-public space below. This area connects the building to the city, as the internal garden becomes visible for exterior onlookers as well. The upper floor of Simplon A features five unique and peculiar penthouse flats that are surrounded by glass walls and private roof gardens.

The Simplon A residential block successfully incorporates unique building materials and techniques in its design, but remains grounded in vernacular architecture through its design principles.

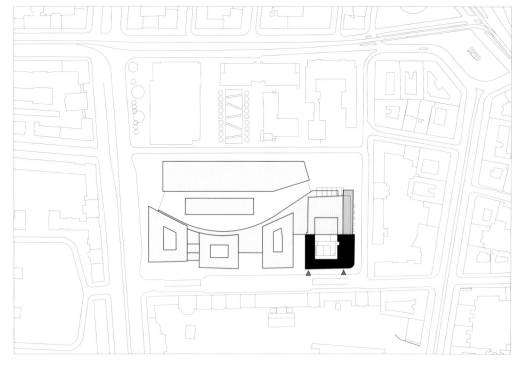

1. The Simplon A project constitutes the residential portion of a mixed-use development situated in southwestern Budapest. The building wraps around the main corner of the two large streets it rests against as this site plan demonstrates.
2–5. Floor plans. The units can be reached through two vertical movement cores, which are placed in the two breakpoints of the U-shaped building. Open-side corridors connect the elevators and stairs through each flat to promote natural ventilation and lighting on both sides.
6. Interior open corridors face the quiet internal garden.

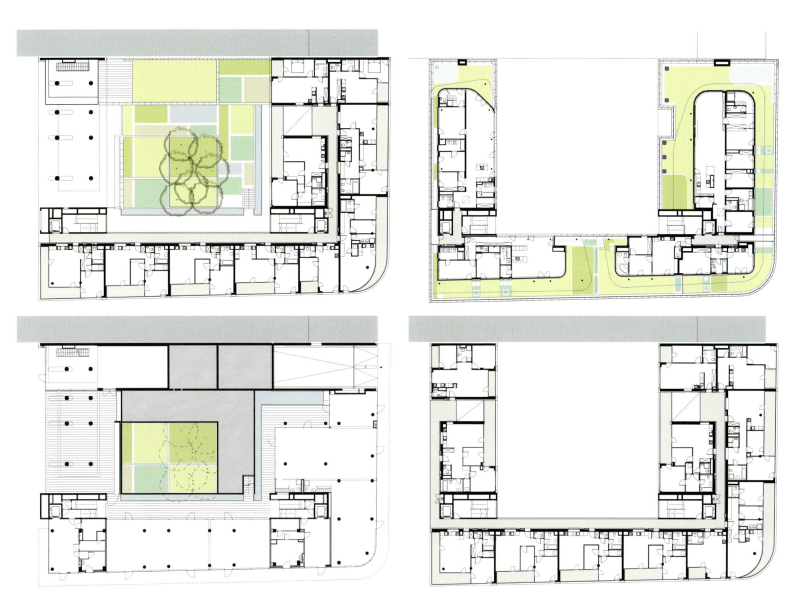

7. Colored glass was used on the façade to include bright and unmixed colors like yellow, orange and red.

8. Each color along the façade marks another residence and also appears at the main door of that particular unit.

9. Each residence is marked in a different color, making the identification of each dwelling simple and playful.

The Mountain, Copenhagen, Denmark
Design: Bjarke Ingels Group (BIG), 2008

The Mountain is an apartment building with unique construction methods which measures 33,000 m² (355,209 sq. ft.) and house 80 units. The goal of the architects while designing the eleven-storey structure was to combine the allure of a suburban backyard with the dense urban housing.

One of the clients' programmatic requests was that the building will have an adequate balance between parking and living spaces. Rather than creating two distinct entities to satisfy the two functions, BIG opted to combine them both in a single edifice with a plan that included 2/3 parking spaces and 1/3 housing. As a result the residents of these 80 apartments will be able to park directly outside their units. The parking area includes 480 spots, and a sloping elevator that travels along the mountain's inner walls.

To generate its layout, the concrete base serves as an underground car park, while the terraced housing is situated immediately above it. As a result, the project includes a unique arrangement of the concrete base to create a shape that resembles a hillside covered by a layer of housing cascading from the eleventh floor to the street. The parking segment is linked to the road, and the cascading housing units are exposed to abundance sunlight. Moreover, each apartment includes a roof garden facing the sun with stellar views.

The method employed by BIG to create this cascading concrete hillside resulted in an exceptional building which includes the benefits above ground greenery. As a result, the roof gardens of each unit contain a private terrace and garden. Particularly rare and unique much like the development itself, the flora selected for the roof gardens includes plants that change character according to the seasons.

To sustain the quality of the roof gardens a self-watering garden system was included. This automated system is synchronized with the date and time of the region to ensure that the gardens remained hydrated. To provide light and fresh air, the only physical separation to exist between the apartments and the gardens is a glass façade with sliding doors.

An interesting choice of materials was also employed along the building's envelop. The north and west façades are covered by perforated aluminum plates, which let in air and light to the parking area. The holes in the façade form a huge reproduction of a mountain. At day the holes in the plates appear black on the bright aluminum, and the gigantic picture will resemble that of a rough photo. At nighttime the façade is lit from the inside and appears as a photo negative since each floor in the parking area has different colors.

Several innovations were presented in the design on The Mountain with the most striking of them is a relation between apartment units and parking spots.

1. The Mountain apartment building is part of a new residential development in the district of Ørestad near Copenhagen.
2. When designing the eleven-storey structure, the goal of the architect was to combine the allure of a suburban backyard with that of a dense urban housing.
3. The Mountain project creates a shape that resembles a hillside covered by a layer of housing cascading from the eleventh floor to the street as demonstrated in this section.

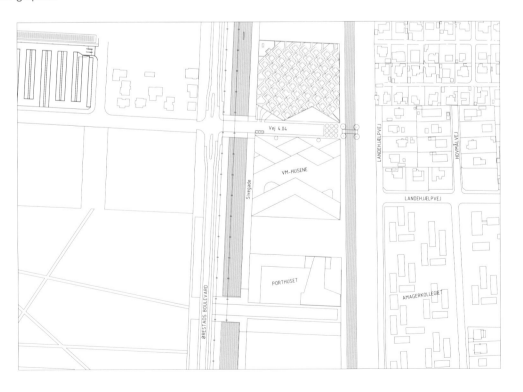

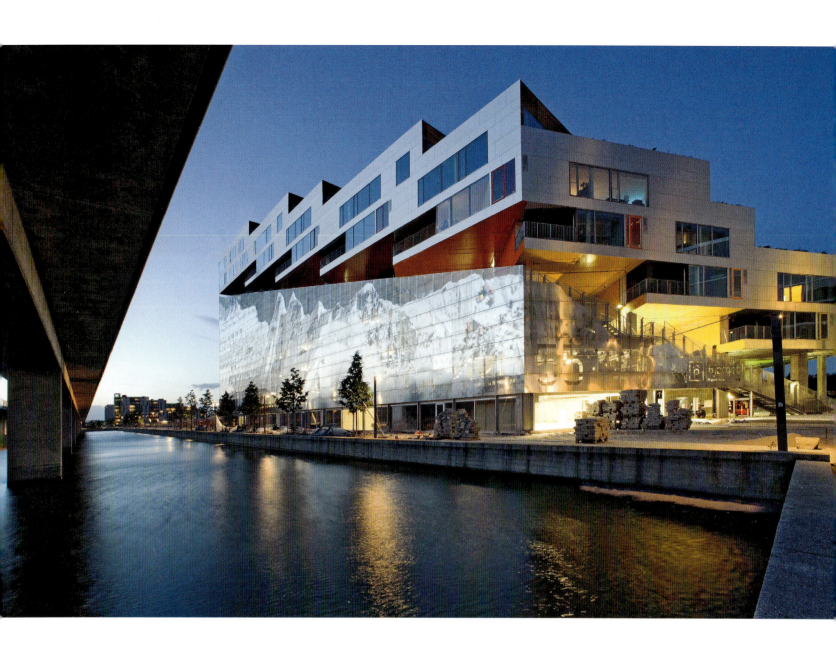

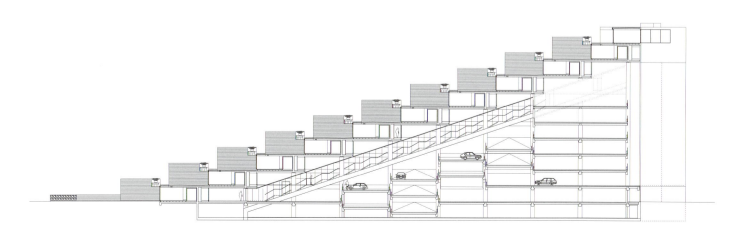

4, 5. The north and west façades are covered by
perforated aluminum plates, which let in air and light
to the parking area. The holes in the façade form a
huge reproduction of a mountain. During the day the
holes in the plates appear black on the bright aluminum. At night, the façade is lit from the inside and
appears as a photo negative since each floor in the
parking area has different colors.

6, 7. Floor plans. The concrete base serves as an
underground parking, while the terraced housing
is situated immediately above it. Each apartment
includes a roof garden facing the sun with stellar
views.

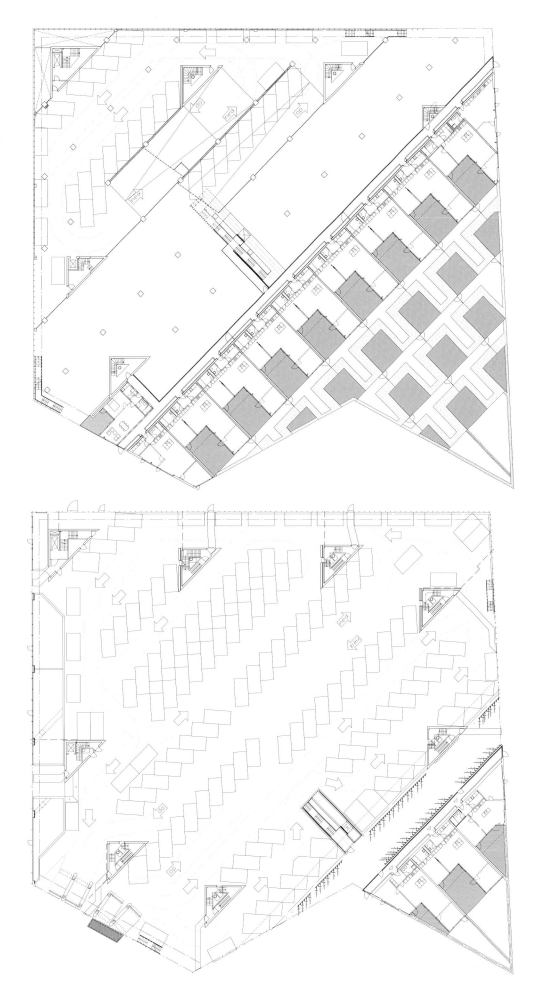

The Wave, Vejle, Denmark
Design: Henning Larsen Architects, 2009

The Wave, an apartment building complex with a floor area of 14,000 m² (150,694 sq. ft.) and 100 residential units, was named after its form. The project is a special combination and choice of building materials and methods, which resulted in a unique structure.

With its striking form, the project stands out as a structural icon while respecting and challenging its location. When selecting a form, the architects kept in mind that the project has a potential to become a landmark for the city. In fact, the development was the recipient of the prestigious Civic Trust Award. According to the British reviewer Michael Webb, The Wave demonstrates how Danish architects are responding to global trends without sacrificing the practicality or well-crafted detailing that have long been a signature of that country.

Seen from a distance, the chosen form and material turns the project a visually constant changing landscape. One of the special characteristics of this building is its modularity. Modular construction, in this case, does not refer to the ability to »plug« every unit into the structure but to the flexibility of each wave crest with reference to the entire project. In fact, during the construction each wave crest was built independently to allow for another to be added at the discretion of the client in the future.

The main materials used along the façades are concrete, glass and steel. During the day, the building and its materials are characterized by the soft movements of the waves reflected in the water surface of the nearby fjord. In contrast, the iconic profile of the Wave appears as a scintillating mountain landscape of light and color at night. As opposed to other traditional apartment units, many of the 100 dwellings are two-storey units oriented to the fjord's water to ensure a remarkable view from all balconies.

In sum, the clear and easily recognizable signature of the building connects the residential area with the sea, the landscape and the town to make a welcome urban and architectural composition.

1. With its striking form, the Wave stands out as a structural icon while respecting and challenging its location near the waterfront of the fjord as seen in this site plan.
2. The iconic profile of the Wave appears as a mountain landscape of light and color at night. Seen from a distance, the chosen form and material of the Wave turns the project into a constantly changing visual landscape.
3. A section showing the structure's vertical movements.

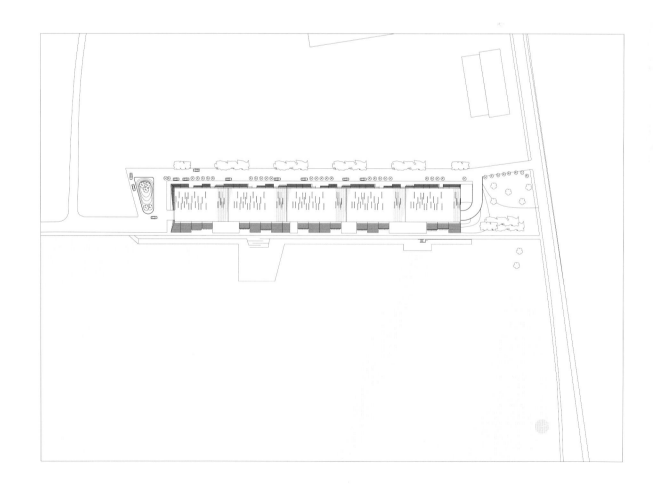

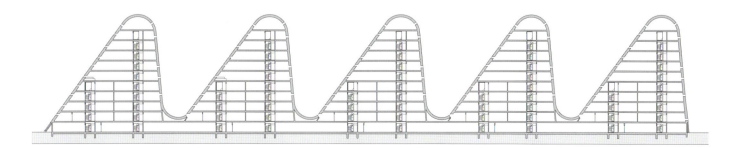

4. View of the living, kitchen and dining areas which enjoy a spectacular lookout as a result of the glass façades.
5–7. Floor plans (due to the building's unique shape, there is a variety of dwelling types including a top floor penthouse).
8. Many of the 100 dwellings are two-storey units oriented to the fjord with a remarkable view from all balconies.

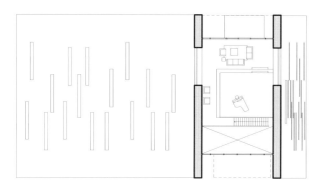

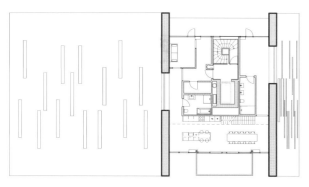

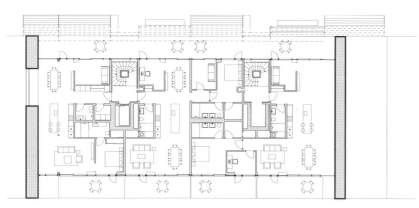

Plaza Europa Tower, L'Hospitalet de Llobregat, Spain

Design: Roldán + Berengué, arqts., 2010

The Plaza Europa residential Tower is a social housing project in a new central zone known as Plaça Europa (Europa Square) a vast open space dedicated to public use. It opens onto the Gran Via, which concentrates approximately 26 other residential and public towers that range in height from 15 to 20 floors. In the recent past, many of these built projects have included social housing blocks like Plaza Europa Tower. The master planning laws for the region include certain architectural constraints, such as a maximum floor dimension of 24 m by 24 m, and a certain height for the first level of the building. Buildings immediately adjacent to Plaza Europa Tower are mostly five storeys tall. As a result, the architect's main concept was to design a building that would blend into the urban fabric of the surrounding context through construction techniques and materials. Therefore, when designing the façade, the materials and form seek to consolidate floors in groups of three in order for the image of the tower to be perceived as a building of only five floors.

Consequently the scale of the windows, according to the law grouping them, is also transforming in frames of 10 m in height and of different thicknesses. The façade is composed of different planes that intersect and recess by varying dimensions. Also, the balconies are situated on every third floor of the building. The interior segment of the building also features this interesting treatment of space. Lengthier frames and corridors avoid vertigo impression because of the integration of intermediate elements that affect the viewer. These elements include doorjambs, windows and balconies. The selection of the elements for the façade's assembly has been done by paying attention to a comparative study of several constructive solutions which evaluated the origin of already recycled materials, its natural origin and the capacity for being recycled at the end of its useful life. Moreover, the selected materials are conscious of the energy expenditure required to make them, and to eventually dispose of them when they whether.

The innovative materials and building techniques of Plaza Europa Tower's allow it to appear as a building of only five storeys, when it is actually composed of 15 levels. In addition, its conscious use of building materials are environmentally beneficial and allow it to become a focal point in this public square.

1. The Plaza Europa Tower opens onto the Gran Via which concentrates approximately 26 other residential and public towers. In the recent past, many of these projects have included social housing blocks like Plaza Europa Tower.
2. Site plan. The buildings immediately adjacent to formal-looking Plaza Europa Tower are mostly five storeys tall.
3, 4. Floor plans. The interior of Plaza Europa features interesting treatment of spaces to include doorjambs, windows and balconies.

pp. 116, 117
5. The architect's main concept was to design a building that would blend into the urban fabric of the surrounding context through construction techniques and materials.
6. The façade is composed of different planes that intersect and recess by varying dimensions. Also, the balconies are situated on every third floor of the building.

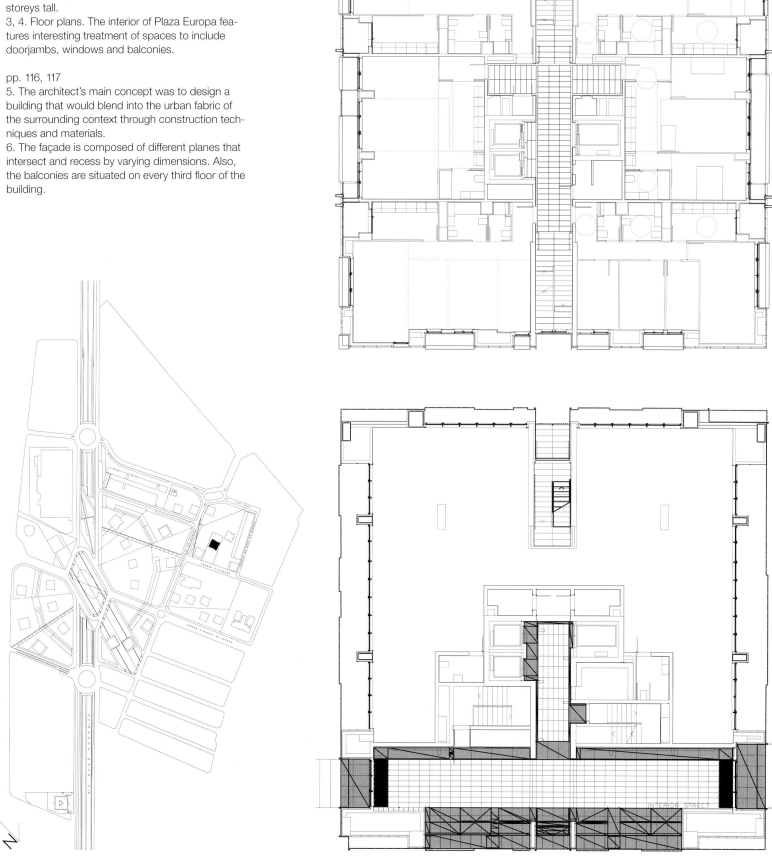

Apartments for seniors and multigenerational arrangements

In recent decades, the proportion of senior citizens has increased more rapidly than any other age bracket. There has also been a significant decrease in the number of young people entering the labor force. This ratio means that health and pension funds will continue to be supported by a relatively smaller number of economically active citizens. It also means that more seniors will need to live or be housed in dwellings that were designed to account for their special needs. This chapter examines apartment buildings that have been designed to house the elderly and multi-generational family units.

Designing buildings for seniors requires foresight about the lifestyle changes and challenges resulting from reduced mobility. An aging population may decide to continue living in their current dwelling or move into smaller units in proximity to social and medical hubs, a place that meets their budget and require less maintenance. The first adjustment strategy involves preparing a new unit for future interior adaptations and additions of specialized components. This begins with a general understanding of the limitations inherent in the aging process including: loss of coordination, impaired vision and reliance on wheelchair for mobility, to name a few.

Overall exertion can be minimized by adhering to universal design principles, which account for the needs of the population at large. These design elements include lower window sills, low beveled thresholds, extended handrails, raised electrical outlets and ergonomically placed cabinets. Reinforced interior partitions in corridors and bathrooms prepare the home for grab bars and railing installation. Design considerations, such as width of doors and access ways, account for the eventual use of a wheelchair.

A second stage of gradual adjustments is administered according to level of impairment. The bathroom and kitchen are target areas for safety and mobility related retrofits. Handheld shower heads are often installed to reduce bending. Commodes, anti-slip surfaces, grab bars, transfer tables and shower benches allow seniors to navigate without assistance. For wheelchair-bound occupants, roll-in showers with flexible curbs replace full tubs. If a patient begins to lose heat sensitivity, temperature controls may be added to ensure his or her safety in the shower or bath. The emphasis here is on occupant safety and independent self-care.

Kitchen work surfaces deserve equal attention in the later years. Higher cabinets may become inaccessible to those struggling with balance and flexibility. Lower storage spaces and pull-out work surfaces alleviate the risks associated with domestic tasks. Counter and sink heights will need to be adjusted for wheel chair users. Automatic shut-off devices should be installed on all appliances, particularly in residences with occupants suffering from dementia.

Subsequent additions may touch on general mobility issues. Arthritic seniors may opt for easy-to-operate door handles over traditional doorknobs. Moreover, wheelchair users will require automatic door openers and exterior entrance ramps. Grab bars, tread nosing and light switches benefit from high-contrast or light emitting coatings for the visually impaired.

Another method of caring for seniors is to house them with younger generations of the same family. A multigenerationalliving arrangements promotes a sustainable lifestyle from both a social and economic perspectives. Elderly persons who live alongside their offspring have the opportunity to maintain an active autonomous or semi-autonomous routine. The younger generation provides emotional security and physical assistance when needed. Multigenerational dwellings require separation of family units such that each household will be able to live independently should they choose so. This also makes the future sale or rent of units possible.

Several arrangements are commonly associated with multi-generational housing. Side-by-side units follow the same form as semi-detached houses and townhouses where both units have the same level access yet they are separated by a partition wall. The spatial relationship between the two main entrances and the removal of certain interior partitions can create communal spaces. Superimposed units are defined by level changes. While one unit has lower level entry, the second can be accessed from an interior or exterior stairway. The elder generation often occupies the lower level floor due to its increased accessibility.

The time of guaranteed placement in assisted living institutions has long since passed. Modern medicine continues to extend average life expectancies. However, it is doubtful that these innovations will overcome the limits of health care facilities and their staff. If seniors remain the fastest growing population bracket, housing solutions for this aging community will become a matter of necessity.

Armstrong Place Senior Housing, San Francisco, California, USA

Design: David Baker Architects, 2011

Armstrong Place is a 116 housing units development for seniors with a floor area of 131,800 m² (1,418,638 sq. ft.) on a former industrial city block. In addition to apartments, the project includes affordable townhouses to prevent seniors from living in isolation. The rental cost of units was meant to meet the affordability level of the elderly in the area and some units' house formerly homeless seniors.

When selecting the site, the developers recognized its proximity to public services making it part of a transit-oriented development along the city's business corridor. Armstrong Place is located a mere block away from a stop of a new light-rail line, a park, and a health center and serves as a community anchor. The apartments overlook the park, the courtyard, or a landscaped mews that runs between the building and the family townhouse development.

In response to the African-American roots of the district, the architects included design elements, which were drawn directly from traditional African textiles and symbols. These textile-inspired paint details combined with various protruding window arrangements, wrap the façade of the building in an interlocking layer of colors and patterns. One of the inner courtyard's walls is inscribed with Ashanti tribal symbols, which represent security, love, hope, power and unity.

Since its completion, Armstrong Place has become a LEED NC accredited development, with the goal of eventually obtaining LEED Gold recognition. The designers included in the project environmental features such as storm-water management, water heater solar based arrays that also light the common spaces, and choice of healthy interiors and materials.

Armstrong Place demonstrates that high quality affordable housing for seniors can be design in the heart of communities one that also integrates cultural aspects.

1. Armstrong Place is located near a new light-rail line stop, a park and a health center to serve as a community anchor.
2. The apartments of Armstrong Place overlook a park, courtyard, and a landscaped mews that runs between the building and a townhouse development.
3, 4. Floor plans. The ground floor includes social spaces and the upper ones a variety of dwelling types and sizes.

pp. 122, 123
5. The architects included design elements which were drawn from traditional African textiles and symbols.
6. One of the inner courtyard's walls is inscribed with Ashanti tribal symbols, which represent security, love, hope, power and unity.

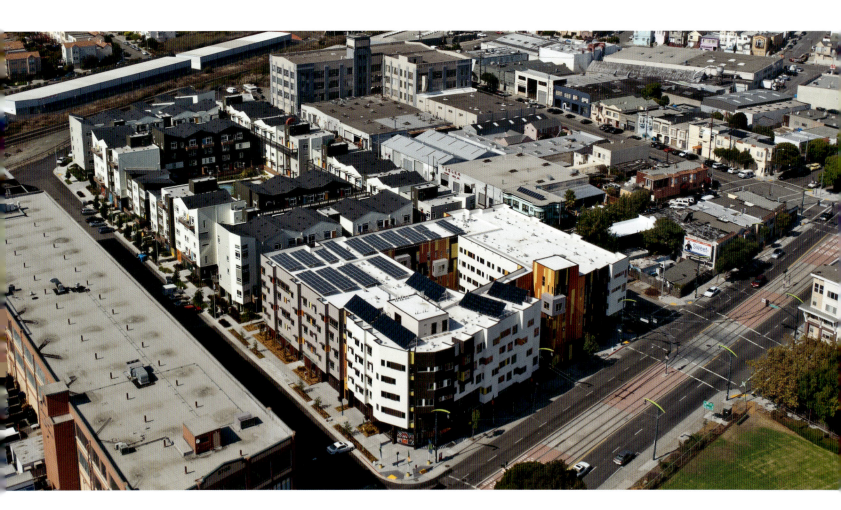

De Dijken 10, Leidschenveen, Netherlands
Design: HVE Architecten, 2010

The De Dijken 10 project house 81 apartments for seniors in four- and five-storey buildings with a floor area of 9,800 m² (105,486 sq. ft.).

Situated in a new district, one of the development's four blocks is a social housing initiative, while the other three are market housing. In conjunction with the client, the architects pondered several design ideas, including elongated compact volumes but ultimately opted to design four distinct buildings. As a result, the segmented structural composition coupled with the delightful green spaces between them contributes to create a matching visual relationship. With input and involvement from future residents, the open spaces got their final shape.

The structure's design has a quasi-industrial appearance. Characterized by bright materials and detailing, the architectural features include metal framings, ceramic tiles, and references to the 1930s Nieuwe Haagse School style. The substructure is decorated with stone baskets filled with sand-colored boulders. A separation between collective courtyards and public spaces is formed by garden walls, which span the perimeter of the project. On the other hand, the super-structure is composed of a red ceramic tile that was selected to resemble the red/brown brick ever so present in the district.

Along its longitudinal direction, horizontal terra cotta bands that extend across parts of the length characterize De Dijken 10. This particular articulation offers human scale and airiness. In addition, it creates an underlying connection between the volumes of blocks. In direct contrast, the transverse façades feature cladding with a significantly lesser number of openings, and traits that enhance the blocks' verticality. As a result, the architects have created an internal dialogue within the senior housing complexes, which speaks to the longitudinal nature of the development. Indoors, the detailed materials are rather modest, mainly featuring stucco and stone. As an innovative way of highlighting the waiting areas for elevators, staggered voids and spaces were utilized. Through the use of these voids, the entrance hall is connected to all the floors above thereby becoming a pleasant area to be in.

The design of De Dijken 10 included innovative and insightful design elements, which transform potentially banal spaces into intriguing ones to create a comfortable place for seniors.

1. Situated in a new district of the city of Leidschenveen, one of the development's four blocks is social housing, while the other three are market dwellings. A separation between common courtyards and public spaces is formed by garden walls, which span the perimeter of the project.
2. The segmented structural composition of each building coupled with the delightful green spaces between them contributes to the creation of a matching visual relationship.
3. While designing the floor plan, the architect took into consideration the needs of people with reduced mobility.

4. The exterior lower wall is decorated with stone baskets filled with sand-colored boulders as shown in this side elevation.
5. To highlight the entrance areas, the spaces were utilized in an innovative way thereby becoming a pleasant space.

John C. Anderson Apartments (JCAA), Philadelphia, Pennsylvania, USA
Design: Wallace Roberts & Todd (WRT), 2014

The John C. Anderson Apartments (JCAA), a six-storeys tall building in Philadelphia includes 56 affordable units, tailored for senior citizens with floor area of 1,618m² (17,424 sq. ft.).

Located in Philadelphia's historic Washington Square West neighborhood, the complex was completed in 2014 through a public-private partnership, between the non-profit organization DMH Fund that focuses on the needs of youth and seniors, and a highly experienced affordable housing developer. Through the organization's involvement, community members were able to have active roles in the design and construction phases of the project. The project is known to be the one of the leading affordable senior housing projects completed in the USA with a high level of community involvement. After such a collaborative effort, it was no surprise that this meticulously detailed structure become a source of communal pride.

On a former parking garage site, one can now see a building with charcoal tone brick and pumpkin color panels exterior. The architectural features of the JCAA made it unique. The building fills the lot almost entirely edging up to the street line, and featuring plenty of glass along the façades to draw city life in. On ground floor, the a lobby and a modest retail space was included. Despite being placed between two nineteen-century townhouses and one of the city's last single-room occupancy hotels, JCAA does not show any signs of historic aspects weighing it down. On the contrary, the architects were attempting to break away from the traditional look, and build a contemporary structure. Consequently, the JCAA senior housing apartments features a trim, and layered façade, which is infused with color and texture. Despite a desire to make this building appear stylistically contemporary, the budget was fairly constrained, a phenomenon all too familiar in affordable housing. However, the designers still felt that the building needed to feel and appear dynamic. The façade is composed of a series of overlapping planes, and an enormous, protruding rectangular bay covered in burnt orange panels. This rectangular protrusion is pierced with an off-center void, treated in black seamed metal. Indoor, each apartment benefits from a generous amount of natural light, in part due to the large, internal courtyard.

The project demonstrates that integration can be made between traditional architecture and cotemporary to also become affordable.

PROGRAM

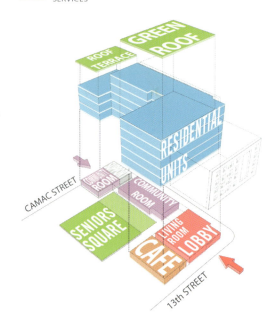

- RECEPTION / LOBBY
- NEIGHBORHOOD CAFE
- COMMUNITY MULTI-PURPOSE ROOM
- RESIDENTIAL : 56 APARTMENTS
- COMMUNAL GREEN SPACES
- SERVICES

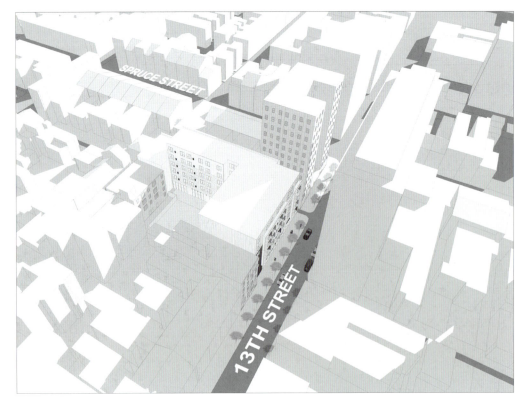

1. Located in Philadelphia's historic Washington Square West neighborhood, the project is known to be the one of the leading affordable senior housing projects in the USA with a high level of community involvement.
2. A diagram featuring the building's main functions.
3. The JCAA senior housing apartment features a layered façade infused with color and texture.
4, 5. Floor plans (some of the building's corridors are double loaded while others are single).

pp. 130, 132
6. The courtyard area creates a tranquil space and offers a view from top units.
7, 8. The common ground floor area enjoys views of the exterior.

Paisano Green Community, El Paso, Texas, USA

Design: Workshop 8, 2012

The Paisano Green Community contains 73 affordable senior housing units with a floor area of 5,142m² (55,357 sq. ft.) in El Paso, Texas. The development was considered an important achievement for this border town due to its environmental features.

Designed by Workshop8, the project is highly sustainable due to its ability to provide low-income public senior housing and the numerous green features it includes. During the design process, the committee responsible for initiating the project received a grant from the American Recovery and Reinvestment Act (ARRA). The design goal was to create safe affordable housing. However, the grant also presented an opportunity to put El Paso on the map as a leader in green architecture.

Workshop8 created a central garden, flanked by four three-storey structures to the west, and a two-storey community center to the east. Connected by a canopy wall, the flats are adequately protected from the potent afternoon sun, winter wind and noise. This gesture also provides a great opportunity to utilize its upper set of beams as a large surface on which photovoltaic panels can be arranged. Distributed across most of the flat roof surfaces, the project includes an impressive 165-kilowatt solar array. The architects' decision to include solar features is an innovative way to exploit the 302 days of sun which El Paso enjoys yearly. The tight building envelope includes R-26 walls, with a hybrid system of insulation that possess minimal thermal bridging. In addition, the majority of the construction materials used was recycled, recyclable, low-maintenance or local. As a result of these features the project became the first net-zero, fossil-fuel free, and LEED platinum senior housing project in the USA.

This development is surrounded by industrial and civic uses which ultimately influenced its function. The designers placed the buildings on the perimeter of the site to create a strong set of edges and to form a protected central garden space providing a serene and secure an oasis like area for seniors.

1. In Paisano Green, a central garden is flanked by four three-storey structures to the west and a two-storey community center to the east. Connected by a canopy wall, the units are adequately protected from the potent afternoon sun, winter wind and noise.
2. The architects' decision to include solar panels like the ones shown on this façade exploits the 302 days of sun which El Paso enjoys yearly.
3. View of the solar panels from the building's interior.

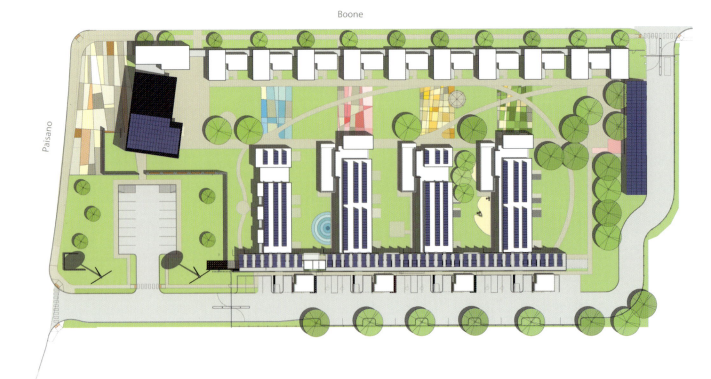

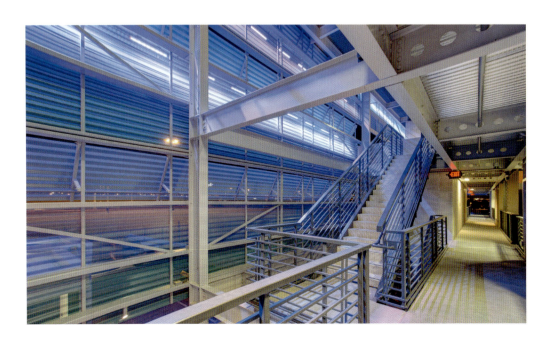

4. A view onto the common open space between the buildings.
5. The common community room for the seniors.
6. The façades were designed with indented opening for protection from the desert sun.

Building with sustainable technologies

With the constant rise in global temperatures, climate change can no longer be ignored. To reverse these phenomena, designers of apartment buildings are integrating sustainable construction strategies in their plans. Such technologies are known to contribute to the reduction of the buildings' ecological footprint and include green roofs and water efficiency, to name a few. This chapter describes these two technologies, illustrating them with buildings that have incorporated them into their design.

Terms such as »green« or »eco« are used to describe roofs where plants are used to improve performance and appearance. This age-old concept has been reintroduced with contemporary technologies to confront the growing environmental challenges associated with conventional roofing. When designing such roofs it is important to determine its »intensity«, or the thickness and type of the vegetation and the protective layers which will depend on the desired use. Those who want minimal vegetation and do not intend to walk on it can use extensive roofs, which are also the most affordable. In contrast, designers who would like to have outdoor roof terraces, edible landscaping and trees are advised to select the intensive or the semi-intensive types.

Extensive green roofs are simple and lightweight, with little plant diversity and low maintenance requirements. In general, their construction does not mandate any additional structural reinforcement due to the minimal substrate depth, which usually ranges between 50 to 150 mm (2 to 6 in.). The semi-intensive green roof is similar to the extensive one, with the only difference being the use of a deeper substrate, 10 to 20 cm (4 to 8 in.), to accommodate a larger range of flora and fauna. This thicker vegetation serves to absorb more rainwater, further cool the roof through evapo-transpiration and acts as a larger thermal mass to more effectively moderate the temperature.

An intensive green roof differs greatly from the previous systems by also being a garden and a terrace. These roofs typically require additional structural support due to the added weight of both people and the thicker substrate needed for the plants and trees. This substrate is composed of thicker soils and organic matter for richer growing conditions. With global concerns over water shortages, conservation and efficiency have become highly important for governments, designers and homeowners. In response, technologies that minimize usage, and recycle waste water without compromising quality or service have been developed. Such tools have also been put to use to create water efficient dwellings.

Water-efficient design can be achieved by focusing on increasing appliance efficiency and decreasing flow rates. Conventional toilets, for example, can be replaced by ones that reduce consumption by over 20 percent. These technologies can be applied to most fixtures and appliances found in the bathroom and the kitchen. As for toilets, there exist four common types: dual-flush, high-efficiency, pressure-assisted and composting toilets. The dual-flush toilet is highly versatile because of its two modes – one for high water conservation and another for standard-sized flush. Pressure-assisted toilets are able to reach even lower levels of water usage. These toilets function by using a build-up of compressed air from the previous flush to create a high-velocity flush.

In addition to reducing water usage in toilets, shower head technologies can be considered. Currently, low-flow shower heads come in either aerating or non-aerating models. Regardless of the fact that they are equally efficient, however, aerating models tend to be the most popular since they use air bubbles to create higher pressure spray. Faucets are another appliance with which homeowners can implement water-saving measures. While most conventional faucets can be retrofitted with aerators to reduce their water consumption, it is also possible to buy those with built-in aerators. These technologies can reduce flow in bathrooms and kitchens by up to 50 percent and can be used for most types of faucets with a small investment.

The last set of appliances that can incorporate water-saving technologies consists of dishwashers and laundry machines. For dishwashers, it is recommended that dwelling units have high-efficiciency models. It is also important to choose appliances with water-saving controls available on the front panel. For laundry, front-loading machines tend to be slightly more efficient in energy and water consumption than top loaders.

With global warming, the need to rethink current methods of consumption, production, of natural resources is ever more apparent. Combining initiatives for greener apartment buildings will help conserve the environment for future generations.

8House, Copenhagen, Denmark
Design: Bjarke Ingels Group (BIG), 2010

8House contains 476 apartments with a floor area of 61,000 m² (656,599 sq. ft.). This mixed-use development includes residential, office spaces and retail areas. Completed in 2010, the complex is situated at the southernmost edge of Copenhagen. As opposed to traditional urban blocks, the architects combined several aspects of a contemporary, lively neighborhood in one structure. Consequently, the place features horizontal layers connected by a continuous promenade and cycling path. It allows people to bike all the way from the street up to tenth level penthouses alongside terraced gardens. In addition, the bowtie shape of the development creates two interior courtyards, separated by the center of the cross, which houses 500 m² (5381 sq. ft.) of communal facilities. At the same location, a 9 m (30 ft.) wide path cuts through the structure, allowing easy flow between the park area in the west to water filled canals in the east. Also, the designers decided to spread the residential and commercial functions of the building horizontally, rather than have them in separate blocks.

The bowtie shape of 8House also mimics the decision to coordinate the habitation and trade functions along a horizontal axis. Furthermore, the apartments are placed at the top while the commercial program unfolds at the base of the building. Interestingly enough, the architects' desire to slice the functions across layers allows them to inherit unique qualities. For example, the apartment units benefit from stellar views, sunlight, and fresh air, while the offices merge with the activities of the street level. Moreover, the general form of the development enhances these inherent qualities, seeing as the shape of 8 House which is literally hoisted up in the Northeast corner and pushed down at the Southwest corner.

The architects also incorporated subtle building technologies, which allow the project to be recognized for its sustainability. Two sloping green roofs totaling 1,700 m² (5,577 sq. ft.) are strategically placed to reduce the urban heat island effect as well as provide a visual identity to the project and tying it back to the adjacent farmlands towards the south.

With the inclusions of the aforementioned aspects, the architects have successfully created a three-dimensional neighborhood. In a conventional context, social life and spontaneous encounters are reserved to the ground floor. However, the project's inherent design and form allow the intermingling between neighbors to extend across all ten floors of the development. In contrast to other high-rise buildings, 8House uses its imposing height to its advantage. In this regard, the architects have strategically created differences in height, which translate to a unique sense of community with small gardens and pathways, reminiscent of an Italian hill town.

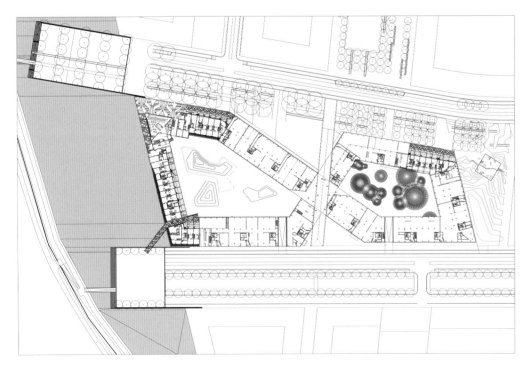

1. The bowtie shape of 8House creates two interior courtyards. At the same location, a 9 m (30 ft.) wide path cuts through the structure, allowing easy flow between the park area in the west and the water-filled canals in the east as showed in this site plan.
2. A night view of 8House. The units benefit from stellar views, sunlight and fresh air, while the offices merge with the street level activities.
3. Floor plan. The project features horizontal layers connected by a continuous promenade and cycling path. It allows people to bike from the street up to tenth level penthouses alongside terraced private gardens.

pp. 140, 141
4. The bowtie shape creates two enclosed and semi-private green public spaces for all to enjoy.
5, 6. Sections showing the private terraces and the external path along the building's perimeter.
7. A view of the common path along the structure's perimeter.
8. The project's inherent design and form allow intermingling between neighbors to extend across all ten floors of the development.

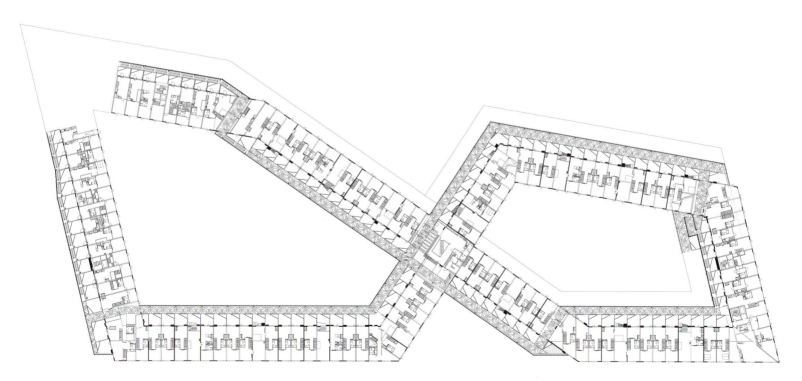

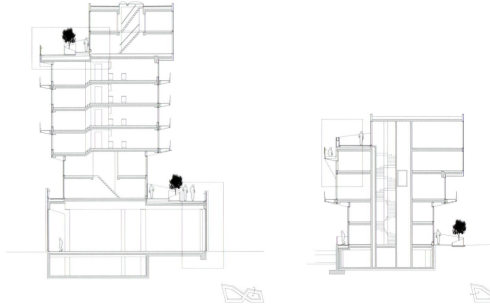

Rita Atkinson Residence, San Diego, California, USA
Design: Valerio Dewalt Train Associates (VDTA), 2010

A recent trend in North American Universities, particularly in California, has been an increased need for student accommodation. Completed in 2010, the Rita Atkinson Residence is a 226 units students' residence apartment building with an area of 20,996 m² (226,000 sq. ft.) in the university of California in San Diego.

The project was built in respond to a projected increase in enrollment along with a shortfall of on-campus residences. Situated near the main entrance to the campus, this nine-storey apartment building soon became a visual icon. It includes 225 two-bedroom units, with an average area of 67 m² (725 sq. ft.) and one three-bedroom manager's unit. The designers wanted to give the structure an urban quality by choosing to employ a concrete frame, a stucco-clad structure, and exposed concrete ceilings and floors.

Part of the building's form stems from the need to be a visual terminus for the future medical campus mall. The site upon which the Rita Atkinson Residence is constructed is approximately 9 m (30 ft.) below the level of the rest of the mall. To achieve this requirement, pragmatic architectural traits have been included while keeping in mind monetary constraints. To remain consistent with the remainder of the campus, this structure consists of two nested, L-shaped towers. The main nine-storey tower points toward the mall to the north and the ocean to the west, while the second seven-storey wing nests with the taller wing to form a three-sided courtyard that offers residents a sheltered outdoor space.

To lighten the building's visual mass, the ends of the wings are elevated and clipped. In addition, the short ends of the wings are colored in the shade of eucalyptus leaves. Several elevations feature a pure white cladding, which is in direct contrast with the green-leafy color of the wings, thereby helping to break the mass of the façade. The designers also incorporated clustered windows so as to create the illusion of a smaller building. The entry to the residence lays three storeys below the level of the mall, decreasing the perceived height of the building from nine to six storeys.

A number of sustainable features were incorporated throughout the design, lending to the building LEED Gold designation. The roof above the third floor is capped with a green courtyard that reduces storm water runoff and provides additional insulation. Moreover, the first floor also includes a bicycle storage room to promote alternate methods of transportation. At one end of each corridor extensive glazing floods circulation spaces with natural light. Notably, the designers took the unique quality of light from the Pacific Ocean under consideration and minimized the number of north facing apartments, thereby allowing the units to be exposed to direct sunlight. In addition, each unit is equipped with operable windows to encourage natural ventilation. Furthermore, a mechanical system that ensures a constant day long low flow of fresh air into the apartments helps remedy the moisture stemming from students hanging their wet swimwear in the apartments.

The Rita Atkinson Residence became an iconic building for the university and is a demonstration that sustainable quality can extend to student housing.

1. The Rita Atkinson Residence consists of two nested, L-shaped towers. The main nine-storey tower points toward the north and the ocean to the west, while the second seven-storey wing nests with the taller wing to form a three-sided courtyard that offers residents a sheltered outdoor space.
2. Floor plan. The building includes 225 two-bedroom units, with an average area of 67 m² (725 sq. ft.) and one three-bedroom manager's unit. The designers took the unique quality of light from the Pacific Ocean into consideration and minimized the number of north-facing apartments, thereby allowing the units to be exposed to direct sunlight.

pp. 143, 144
3. The building forms a sheltered semi-private courtyard for the students to enjoy.
4. View of one of the common rooms that enjoy sunlight and a view of the exterior.
5. The entrance to the Rita Atkinson Residence.

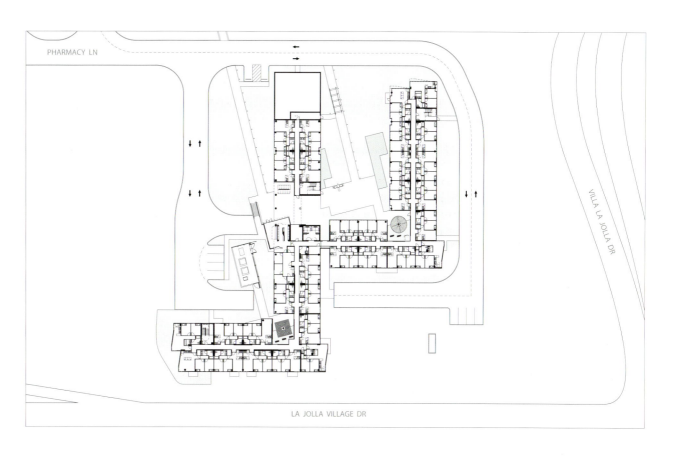

PHARMACY LN

VILLA LA JOLLA DR

LA JOLLA VILLAGE DR

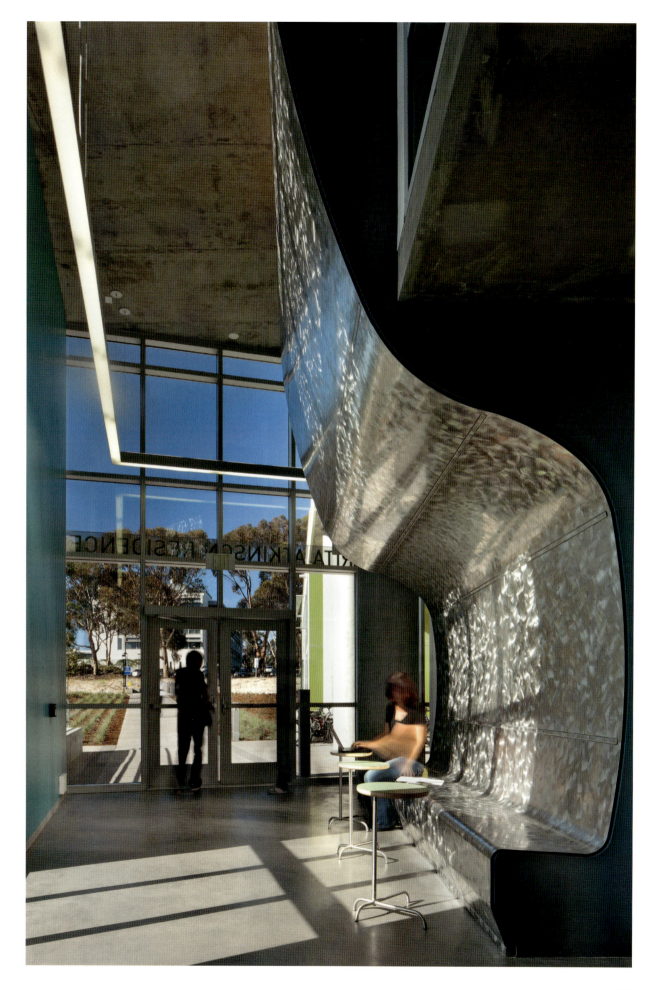

Seven27 Apartments, Madison, Wisconsin, USA
Design: Valerio Dewalt Train Associates (VDTA), 2014

The Seven27 apartment building in Wisconsin has a floor area of 16,420 m² (176,749 sq. ft.) and house 117 luxury apartments on four levels.

When given the design of the Seven27 Apartments project, the firm was asked to develop a luxury building which would also maximize the site's potential. Prior to the construction the 0.6 hectare (1.7 acre) site, it served as a storage yard for a local general contractor. The challenge attributed to this lot was coordinating an appropriate response to the four adjacent sites. On the north edge, the lot encounters two historic loft apartment buildings. Along the south edge, an underutilized city park is cemented in the landscape, providing views to the Monona Bay and Lake Monona. The east edge features the heavily traveled South Commuter bike path, while the west side harbors the historic Bassett neighborhood.

In addition to providing splendid responses to their adjacent sites, the Seven27 apartments also include 20 more units than previously proposed. The design for the building – a U-shaped plan with varying height wings – is oriented toward the south for views of the bay and lake, as well as optimum exposure to daylight and natural ventilation. Along the west façade, the height of the Seven27 decrease to three storeys with masses shaped similar to small houses to mimic the residences across the street in the Bassett neighborhood. In direct relationship to the general U-shape, the constituent wings create a pleasant landscape courtyard, which is ultimately an extension of the abutting city park. As a result, the Seven27 Apartments are characterized by a multitude of green spaces in the center, and a splendid green roof and terrace that covers the underground car park.

To form a dialogue with the adjacent historic Tobacco Lofts, Seven27's design relates to that of its neighbors via building height, massing and materiality. Therefore, it features a four-storey tan-colored brick façade that mediates the height of the two loft warehouse buildings with their cream colored masonry. As a response to the bike path in the east, the architects located Seven27's longest wing to echo the longitudinal style of the Tobacco Lofts.

Throughout the project, one can notice the embedded subtle sustainable core philosophies. These include features such as rain gardens, which collect outfall from the roof leaders and allow it to permeate back into the water table. As previously mentioned, a large green roof occupies the covered garage and is designed to seamlessly merge into the adjacent terrain, while providing a recreation and gathering area for the residents. To benefit from the site's proximity to the downtown area and bike path, the architects equipped the structure with more bike storage and a reduced vehicle parking area, a gesture not always a common in such projects. The highly efficient floor plans employed in the units seek to reduce the building's overall footprint. Also, large high performance glazing windows are located in all apartments, allowing for daylight to penetrate, regardless of the view. Moreover, these efficient windows promote natural ventilation throughout the project.

Valerio Dewalt Train Associates have created a modern apartment building which maximizes the site's potential and also includes green features and building technologies to become a true sustainable development.

1. The design of Seven27 Apartments – a U-shaped plan with varying height wings – is oriented toward the south for views of the bay and lake, as well as optimum exposure to daylight and natural ventilation.
2. To respect the adjacent historic Tobacco Lofts, Seven27's design relates to that of its neighbors via building height, massing and materials. Therefore, it features a four-storey tan-colored brick façade that mediates the height of the two loft warehouse buildings with their cream-colored masonry.
3. Floor plan. The Seven27 Apartments are characterized by a multitude of green spaces in the center, and a splendid green roof and terrace that covers the underground car park.

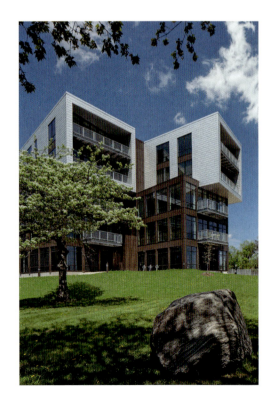

4. View of one of the terraces.
5. View of the exterior from the kitchen. Large high-performance glazing windows were used in all the apartments allowing for daylight to penetrate.

Stadhaus M1, Freiburg, Germany

Design: Barkow Leibinger – Frank Barkow, Regine Leibinger, 2013

The Stadhaus M1 in Freiburg contains 58 apartments and a hotel with 48 rooms with a floor area of 6,668m² (71,773 sq. ft.).

The sustainable development is located near the entrance to the Vauban quarter of the city that is car free. The hotel and the apartment building are linked by a continuous roof and façade. The hotel stands slightly taller than the apartment building and is faced the street, while the residential units are situated at the rear. As a result of the gap between both structures, the architects created a green »pocket-park«. This space widens towards the south and forms a path between the buildings and a connection to the public circulation and greenroom fronting the buildings. Consequently, this architectural gesture lets more daylight enter both buildings to soften their mass.

Along the façades of this mixed-use project, the architects utilized materials and technologies that promote sustainable architecture. In essence, the façades are composed of relatively low-tech materials, which save both energy and cost. Highly insulated wood with triple glazing with integrated retractable louvered sunscreens was employed along the exterior façades of these structures. Due to additional exposure to sunlight, the southern façades were treated with additional care. These southern façades are occupied by loggias and balconies, and are additionally protected by front climbing plants on steel cables. This layer of planting shades the interiors in the summer while allowing warming sun through in the winter. On the other hand, the north facing façades are clad in vertical cedar wood-fins, which served to further unify the visual appearance of both buildings.

In terms of construction materials, the development features a passive energy standard achieved by a structural concrete skeleton frame that includes floor slabs, cores, and columns for fire protection with a non-load bearing insulated prefabricated wood frame infill panel system. The concrete floor slabs are extremely beneficial since they provide added thermal mass while the thin profile of the wood frame walls increases the floor area of each unit.

The architects also employed sustainable features on the roof which is composed of standing seam metal with photovoltaic cells in between. As a result of these features, the units have a transmission heat-loss coefficient 30 percent below the permissible limit, while the primary energy requirement is 70 percent below the permissible level. As a result, the apartment building meets the Freiburg Energy-Efficiency-House Standard 40, based on the internationally used passive house standards. A highly efficient ventilation system with a high heat recovery rate, in combination with a high building density, helps avoid uncontrolled ventilation heat loss.

The inclusion of the above noted technologies in the Stadhaus M1 made it highly energy efficient to help mediate global environmental concerns and a need for conservation.

1. The Stadhaus M1 is located near the entrance to the Vauban quarter of the city of Freiburg. As a result of the gap between both structures, the architects created a green »pocket-park«. This space widens towards the south and forms a path between the buildings and a connection to the public circulation and greenroom fronting the buildings.
2, Sections. The hotel stands slightly taller than the apartment building and face the street, while the residential units are situated at the rear. Both are linked by a continuous roof and façade.
3–5. Floor plans of the apartment building (left) and the hotel (right).

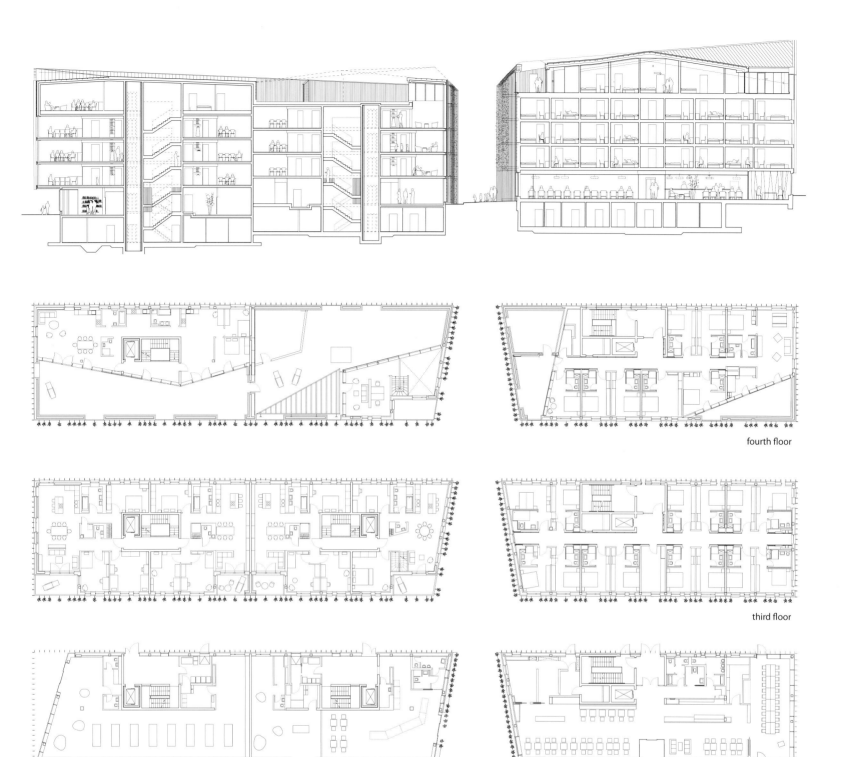

fourth floor

third floor

ground floor

151

6. The southern façades include loggias and balconies and are additionally protected by front-climbing plants on steel cables.

7. The façades are composed of relatively low-tech materials, which save both energy and cost. Highly insulated wood, triple glazing, and integrated retractable louvered sunscreens were employed along the exterior façades of these structures.

8. The buildings feature a passive energy standard achieved by a structural concrete skeleton frame that includes floor slabs, cores, and columns for fire protection with a non-load-bearing insulated prefabricated wood frame infill panel system.

9. A view of a hotel room.

Designing for live-work arrangements

The surge of live-work arrangements, also known as »telecommuting«, can be attributed to the development of digital communication and to the advantages that one has by setting up such an office. Working from home offers a sense of freedom and flexible time management. It also eliminates the cost, stress and loss of time associated with commuting, leaving more time for family and leisure activities. Another rationale touches on the economic benefits of working at home. These hybrid dwelling units allow the home and work place to be financed under a single mortgage as opposed to renting office space separately. This chapter outlines and illustrates the design principles of apartment buildings that include live-work arrangements.

In general, a home office is not simply a spare bedroom with a desk or a nook with a computer. This spatial typology requires a deeper understanding of the type of work being carried out, as well as the temperament of the individual(s) inhabiting the space. When designing a home office, it is important to consider the surrounding context. This often involves a reflection on the desired ambiance and nature of work. One homeowner may wish to achieve complete seclusion, whereas another may find comfort in opportunities to socialize outside of work.

Within the dwelling unit, it becomes important to differentiate between the »live« and »work« spaces. Without proper visual, spatial and acoustical separation, the distractions of domestic life are unavoidable – no matter how focused is the individual. Despite the decision to work from home, there still exists a desire to »go to work«.

One of the primary tools that are used to create work spaces is separation. Some designers have solved this by using passageways or staircases. If a larger office for multiple employees is needed, it is common to designate an entire level. If the occupant wants to have a closer connection between the office and family spaces, then a split-level design can be suggested. This vertical division also creates a visual separation, yet permits communication among household members. At times, noise can become a distraction and therefore the split level is only recommended in quieter situations. For smaller units, interior dividers or partitions that form work stations can also be used. These dividers can be moved around to reconfigure the work areas.

These hybrid living spaces should also be capable of anticipating and accepting change. Depending on the nature of the business, home offices may experience expansion to include additional employees or equipment. Double height spaces, for example, create opportunities to insert a mezzanine for storage or additional work stations. If the occupant expects to receive clients, it may be necessary to add a second entrance or waiting area so that visitors may access the office directly without passing through the living area.

Beyond separating workspaces, there are other methods to improve working conditions in an office. For example, open plan allows for spontaneous discussions and ideas to emerge. Separating work spaces from one another in an attempt to increase the efficiency may lead to a disruption of communication. Establishing distinct activity zones within the office is also a tool used by designers to create environments which encourage workers to move around. An office can feel open, which can be achieved by having two-storey spaces.

Placing offices near the façade with the most sun exposure is also important since letting in ample natural light enhances productivity and well-being. Windows in those rooms should be equipped with blinds to reduce extreme brightness and glare, and surface materials should preferably be non-reflective. In addition, ambient lighting for general illumination should be paired with task lighting in areas where reading, writing or hands-on work occurs. Some professions may also require security doors to safeguard valuable equipment.

Locating the entrance to an office is another important decision a designer has to make. In some cases, the office may have its own independent entrance to allow maximum separation. This is usually done when the office has multiple employees. In other cases, the office can share an entrance with the residence. Although there is a lot of versatility in entrances' design, most designers argue that there should only be a single entrance into a workspace for better internal circulation.

The design of live-work environments is a rapidly evolving area. Due to on-going economic shifts and further development in digital communication working at home is likely to become more common and as a result apartment building design will have to consider this trend.

Arena Apartments, South Brisbane, Australia
Design: Ellivo Architects, 2014

The Arena Apartments development is example of a design for live-work arrangement that features 191 units in twelve-storey towers with a floor area of 4,400 m² (14,436 sq. ft.).

Located in South Brisbane, the Arena development sits on an elevated site with a northeast orientation that offers an exceptional view of the city. The building was designed in response to the site's spatial constraints and views to include two separate towers and podium that create and define a semi-public courtyard. The designers intended this central courtyard to be a significant node of the project. Therefore, it incorporates public café and restaurant spaces, residents' recreational facilities and private courtyards. The towers are rising above the central courtyard and twisted at ninety degrees to the podium to optimize the city-facing views.

Large »chopstick« columns that extend down through the courtyard sit on structural points in the basement support to both towers. To redefine conventional notions attributed to apartment buildings, the designers altered the route of pedestrians who wishes to enter the complex. As opposed to entering each tower from the street, all traffic is redirected through the courtyard and the entrance to the building is granted via an internal street which also promotes social interaction.

The podium and tower elements in each building are differentiated by not only their formal expression but also by their material selections. Throughout the podium areas, the architects chose to employ mainly brick, tile and screening elements. In addition, the extensive use of glass and aluminum details enclosed within the solid frame provides the building with a clear expression. High-quality finishing details such as gallery style track lighting, homogenous commercial vinyl plank flooring and full wall glazing to living areas are also incorporated.

As a way of responding to the social requirement of live-work housing, the Arena Apartments offers an extensive range of dwellings types. These vary in size, and arrangement to satisfy each user's particular lifestyle. Therefore, residents who work extensively from their home would benefit from choosing one of Arena's plan layouts that includes a workspace within the living space of the home or slightly distanced from it. The incorporation of a public café within the development's semi-private courtyard act as a space for residents to perform lighter clerical tasks when they are away from their live-work units.

In sum the Arena Apartments project was configured to satisfy diverse live-work lifestyles based on the discretion of the architect and the desires of the client to form a unique composition.

1. The Arena project sits on an elevated site with a northeast orientation that offers an exceptional view of the city. The project incorporates public café and restaurant spaces, residents' recreational facilities and private courtyards.
2. The building was designed in response to the site's spatial constraints and views to include two separate towers and podium that create and define a semi-public courtyard.

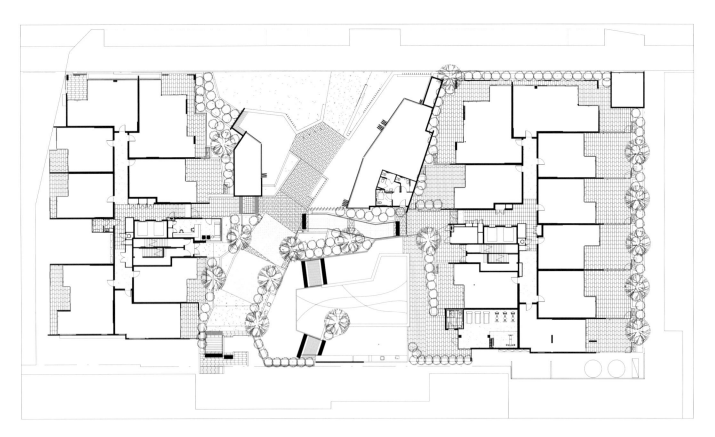

3. View of a kitchen.
4, 5. Floor plans. The Arena Apartments offers an extensive range of dwellings types. These vary in size and arrangement to satisfy each user's particular lifestyle. Therefore, residents who work extensively from their home would benefit from choosing one of Arena's plan layouts that includes a workspace within the living space of the home or slightly distanced from it.
6. High-quality finishing details such as gallery-style track lighting, plank flooring and full-wall glazing to living areas were incorporated in the design.

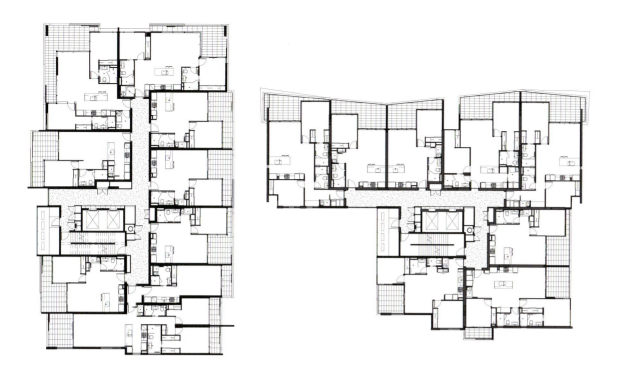

Levent Loft, Istanbul, Turkey

Design: Tabanlioglu Architects, Melkan Gürsel & Murat Tabanlioglu, 2007

The Turkish firm Tabanlıoglu Mimarlık designed the Levent Loft development, a live-work project that features 144 units with a floor area of 3,900 m² (12,795 sq. ft.).

Beyond creating an aesthetically pleasing design, lofts apartment have become a way of life for many urban dwellers. To that effect, the architects sought to employ characteristics that echo an open plan concept with a seemingly industrial tone and open interiors. Located on a narrow site, the building was formally a factory. While maintaining the existing concrete frame, the structure has taken on a new lease on life as an up-market residential enclave. The existing structure set the tone for the new buildings which includes a twelve-storey block at the front, an eight-storey at the rear, and a five-storey coupling link in between. The architects used the existing form to dictate the linear nature of the new. The sizes of the live-work apartments range from 68 m² (731 sq. ft.) to 182 m² (1,959 sq. ft.) with the larger units benefiting from added luxuries like terraces and roof gardens.

The layout, size and type of each unit dictated the make-up of the occupants. For example, the apartments with an elongated plan may not be suited for the growing requirements of family life, but may appeal to single people or couples without children. To reinforce the loft aesthetic, the designers introduced concrete columns, exposed ductwork, floor-to-ceiling operable windows and pine floors. Moreover, the bedrooms have movable dividers that double as storage space. Additional storage required by residents is available in the basement along with parking. To reinforce the idea of a community composed of diverse individuals, the façade was designed to resemble an assortment of boxes. The projecting bays, with their shifting geometries, allow people to readily identify their own space from the outside. Interestingly, the curtain system allows for a range of colors to reflect from inside.

In addition to satisfying the living requirements, the architects intended for this project to have a notable social venue. As a result, the apartments were designed to be private and self-contained but not isolated. The entrance is made through the lobby, designed as the essential meeting place where the residents have a chance to get to know their neighbors. To further enhance the essence of the design, the front lobby contains a restaurant/bar, while the rear block features a swimming pool, a gym, and spa that allow residents enjoying a steam bath to view a landscaped »Zen« garden.

The Levent Loft project represents a significant example of successful space that satisfies both live-work requirements and creates a high quality social venue.

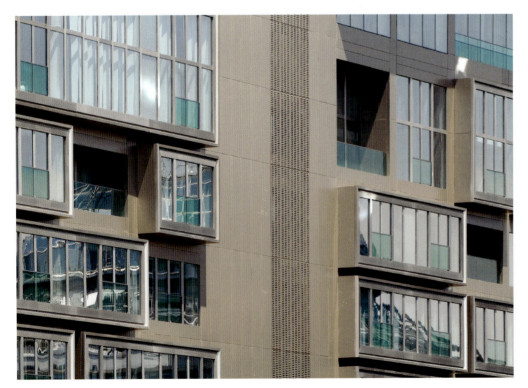

1. Located on a narrow site, the building was formerly a factory. While maintaining the existing concrete frame, the structure has taken on a new lease on life as an up-market residential enclave.
2. The existing structure set the tone for the new buildings which includes a twelve-storey block at the front, an eight-storey block at the rear, and a five-storey link in between. The architects used the existing form to dictate the linear nature of the new.
3. Section/elevation. The architects sought to employ characteristics that echo an open plan concept with industrial features and open interiors.

pp. 162, 163
4. The front lobby of the building contains a restaurant, while the rear block features a swimming pool, a gym, spa and a landscaped »Zen« garden.
5. The elevator lobby of each floor was designed as a meeting place where the residents have a chance to get to know their neighbors.
6. Interior view of a two-storey unit. To reinforce the loft aesthetic, the designers introduced concrete columns, exposed ductwork, floor-to-ceiling windows and pine floors. Moreover, the bedrooms have movable dividers that double as storage space.

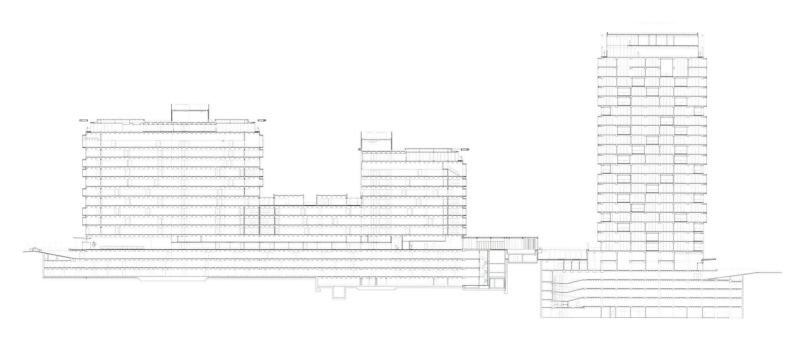

Trenue Tower, Seoul, South Korea
Design: Mass Studies, 2009

The Asian economic boom has made live-work housing very favorable in that region. In 2009, the design firm Mass Studies completed the S-Trenue Tower which includes residential and commercial spaces, harboring the essentials of a live-work environment.

As opposed to designing a simple tower the architects were interested in developing a project that would appropriately respond to the site and its surroundings. Consequently, vertical elements were included to feature three slim towers. Visually, the central core tower, the adjoined street-side tower, the adjoined rear tower and the podium form an »L« that continues as one element reaching a height of 36 floors. The designers decided to use reinforced concrete in the core tower, and steel construction for the other two. With the central core tower, the slimmer steel towers lean at varying angles to maintain structural soundness. These intriguing angles create space between the structures which result in unique outdoor areas that also serve as an extension of the indoor live-work spaces.

Some 32 bridges span across the gaps and connect all three towers structurally and functionally. Each of these bridges has a balcony and greenery on either side, creating pleasant gardens suspended in mid-air. These semi-private spaces extend to the lower four floors of commercial space, an atrium garden, escalator hall and other common areas for rest and transit, which allow the space to remain active. The project is comprised of seven underground levels and 36 upper levels with a floor area of 39,899 m² (130,902 sq. ft.). While the parking and mechanical rooms occupy five basement levels, amenities and commercial spaces are located in the basement's first level all the way to superstructure's fourth floor.

Floors levels five to 36 feature 113 live-work housing units in a variety of layouts and sizes to satisfy a wide variety of residents' requirements. As noted above, many of the embedded public spaces serve as extensions of the live-work units into the outdoor realm. In addition, a 100 m (328 ft.) wide street park has been included along the main level to enhance the presence of greenery within the development.

In addition to creating a building that responds to a new lifestyle trend, the firm Mass Studies also developed a project that sets itself apart from other towers in Asia thanks to its remarkable form and function.

1. Site plan. The architects developed a project that appropriately responds to the site and its surroundings in the heart of Seoul, South Korea.
2–4. Floor plans. Some 32 bridges span the gaps and connect all three towers structurally and functionally. Each of these bridges has a balcony and greenery on either side, creating pleasant gardens suspended in mid-air. These semi-private spaces extend to the lower four floors of commercial space, an atrium garden, escalator hall and other common areas for rest and transit, which allow the space to remain active.

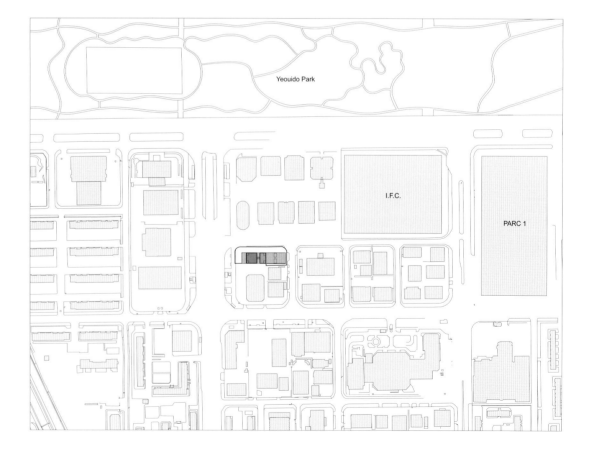

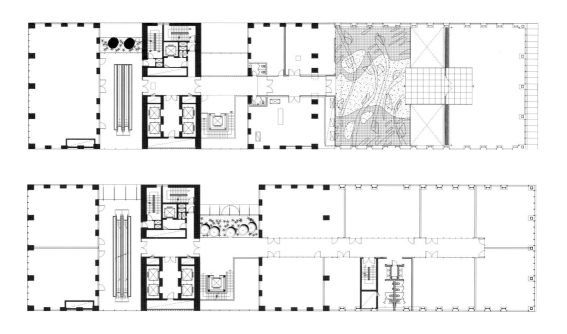

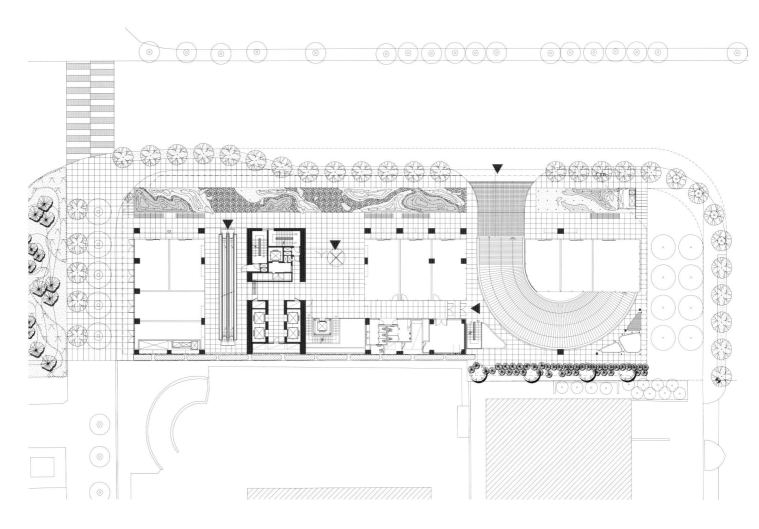

165

5. Visually, the central core tower, the adjoined street-side tower, the adjoined rear tower and the podium form an »L« that continues as one element reaching a height of 36 floors.
6. Many of the interior spaces extend the live-work units into the outdoor realm as shown in this interior view.
7. A view from one of the mid-air terraces into the distant urban area.

Flexible interiors and micro-units

Rising housing and heating costs, the emergence of the non-traditional small household and an increase in the number of seniors have contributed to interest in small and flexible dwellings. Small units can arbitrarily be defined as those with a floor area not exceeding 56 m² (500 sq. ft.). Common in European and Asian cities, their popularity has been rising rapidly in other parts of the world. This chapter outlines design principles of small, flexible apartments which are also known as micro-units.

To be functional, small apartments must be carefully designed as minor decisions can have a large impact on their use. Light, boundaries, circulation, choice of materials and furnishings are some design tools that can expand spatial perception. Therefore, a good design should not only be flexible and efficient, but also avoid simplicity and dullness. Moving away from a more traditional definition of space bound by walls, small dwellings require a looser differentiation of programmed areas and tend toward single open spaces within which multiple activities may occur. One of the strategies employed to improve the spatial perception of an apartment is to increase natural light by proper placement of windows. In urban areas, privacy and property regulations present a unique challenge to designers who have to mitigate between public and private spaces. Solutions to these problems can be introduced by using curtains or shutters to separate between the outdoors and the indoors. Also, easily accessible rooftop spaces can be used for outdoor seating, for example.

Natural light can create a distinct character in a building through its interplay with materials, textures and colours which can break up boxy rooms or help spaces flow into each other. Therefore, it can be assumed that these light-material reactions can be artfully employed to create a diverse interior character which expands the perceptual depth of a home beyond its actual size.

Artificial lights can also play a role in improving the perception of space in an apartment during night time. It can be used to define spaces and create more flexible interior arrangements. Directing light onto works of art can prevent indoor monotony for example. Some designers also favor the reaction of light hitting white walls. Since white walls can reflect the hues of whatever light strikes them, they have the ability to make the home seem larger than it really is.

Interior arrangement is also an important aspect. Partitions, some of which can be flexible, tend to enclose a space while open floor plans increase its use. It can therefore be suggested that spatial overlap between different functions can reduce the need for single purpose spaces, such as hallways, and create a plan in which spaces flow into each other and can be used as multipurpose areas. This can potentially increase the space's versatility and efficiency. Open floor plans also let light from windows travel freely throughout the house.

When partitions must be installed, transparent ones are recommended since they still permit the dispersal of light. Moveable partitions, or sliding panels, are also useful in defining spaces since they allow one to temporarily redefine small spaces according to need. Lastly, an open floor concept with large exterior openings permits views of the outside which can increase the perception of a house's size. Increasing the floor height can greatly expand space without enlarging the floor area.

Another tool used by designers to define spaces without cluttering them is built-in storage. A sizable amount of space is commonly taken up by »stuff«, such as seldom-used furniture and single-purpose items. Since having storage in a small house is critical, designers can create hidden storage places in walls or under beds. Some designers have introduced dish closets and clothes racks in the ceiling which descend with a gentle push. Furniture can also be made more space efficient by embedding it into the structure. Beds and fixtures can be folded into the walls when not in use. Furthermore, items can have multiple uses, rather than a single one. Shower heads can, for example, be swivelled to become kitchen sink taps if needed and storage cabinets can be double sided. When designed properly, built-ins can reduce clutter without compromising functional aspects.

Small, flexible unit design has made large advances and has further potential as technology keeps evolving. Its proliferation holds several societal advantages, such as offering affordable housing solutions and reducing environmental impacts.

Herzberg public housing, Vienna, Austria
Firm Name: AllesWirdGut Architektur + feld72, 2011

The Herzberg public housing complex is an apartment building with a total area of 20,212 m² (217,560 sq. ft.) that was designed to accommodate various types of families.

Designed by AllesWirdGut Architektur + feld72, the main goal of this project is to create a built environment that combines a multitude types of residences into one given neighborhood to facilitate different ways of life. The architects incorporated this approach on both a macro-urban level and micro-architectural level; taking into consideration site planning issues as well as pertaining to details within the building's structure, incorporated this approach. As a result, the site is organized in a rather interesting fashion. The Herzberg public housing complex is comprised of several different pavilions like volumes that represent different urban typologies. One portion of the site contains several point-block buildings scattered across it, while the other end holds a larger residential block with access onto a courtyard, the street, and a plaza with multi-family townhouses.

The diversity of pavilions across the site mediates the difference in urban fabric between the East, a shopping mall, and West, small-scale single-family homes, delimitations of the development. As their height increases, the buildings throughout receive a terraced-treatment, which creates different living and outdoor conditions from floor to floor. Furthermore, this sensibility on the macro and micro scale of the project support the living styles of various families. Moreover, the architectural result is the creation of a project that features a wide range of apartment types; these span from the single-person rooftop apartment with a large terrace to blended flexible family apartments with living rooms from which one or two temporary bedrooms may easily be partitioned off if needed, and to assisted-living homes for children without families. The development's façades receive a unique treatment, where each level is highlighted by a tone of green, which becomes paler as it proceeds to the rooftop. Each pavilion's top floor features a bright white color, signaling the end of the hues of green. As a result, the color design re-unifies the resultant diversity into one coherent neighborhood and provides it with an urban identity of its own.

The Herzberg public housing project emphasizes that different types of families can be accommodated within a diverse urban fabric through innovative architectural design.

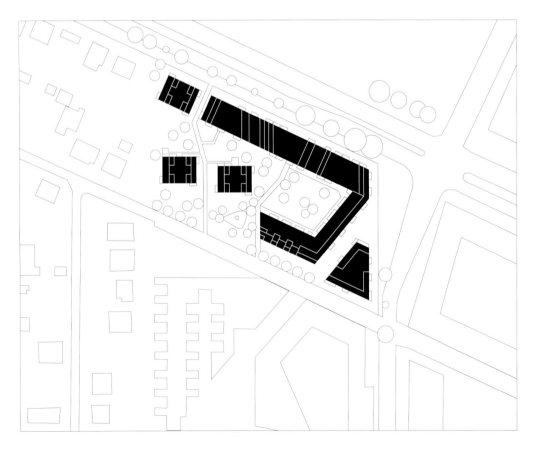

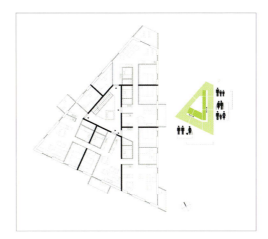

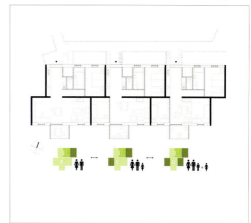

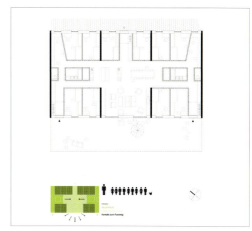

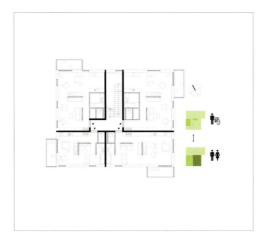

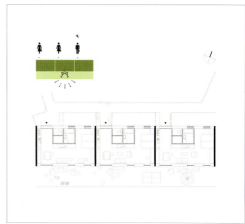

1. Site plan. The Herzberg public housing complex is comprised of several different pavilions like volumes that represent different urban typologies. One portion of the site contains several point-block buildings scattered across it, while the other end holds a larger residential block with access onto a courtyard, the street, and a plaza with multi-family townhouses.

2–8. Floor plans. The design creates different living and outdoor conditions to accommodate the lifestyles of various families. The result is a project that features a wide range of apartment types that span the single-person rooftop apartment with a large terrace to flexible blended family apartments with living rooms from which one or two temporary bedrooms may easily be partitioned off if needed.

9. The diversity of pavilions across the site mediates the difference in urban fabric between the East, a shopping mall, and West, small-scale single-family homes.
10. A view of an interior courtyard.
11. Stairs leading from the units into the courtyard.
12. As their height increases, the buildings throughout receive a terraced treatment, which creates different living and outdoor conditions from floor to floor.
13. A view of a residential space with split-level interior.

Shopping-roof apartments, Bohinjska Bistrica, Bohinj, Slovenia
Design: OFIS Arhitekti, 2006

The shopping-roof apartments is a development that includes dwelling units with flexible interior spaces. The project houses 46 apartments on four levels and has a floor area of 4,200 m² (90,000 sq. ft.). The design is intriguing since the initial condition set by client was for a new shopping mall to be built on top of a former one. However, the new plans used the old shopping mall's roof as the place for the new apartments.

The project is located in the alpine area of Lake Bohinj with breathtaking views of the surrounding mountains. As a result, the organization of the housing and their façades is directed towards these views. Consequently, the wooden façade along the forefront was made transparent with panoramic windows. On the other hand, the side façade is closed and the windows open onto balconies that were inserted into the structure's volume.

Interestingly, the stepped profile of this flexible apartment building traces the silhouette of the landscape in the background. Along the western façade, the development is exposed to strong winds and heavy snow. Subsequently, the openings are along enclosed balconies and this side features a rather monochrome color pattern gray slate. Also, the L-shaped volume encloses an inner communal garden that is the roof of the shopping mall. Conversely, the courtyard façade is warm, open and composed of wooden verticals pieces with a soft rhythm and local larch wood is used in a diagonal vernacular pattern for the roof and the façade. The idea of transparency is omnipresent in this building through vertical wooden elements that form the balcony walls and façade panels. On the other hand, the shopping mall's façade includes steel and glass panels. The flexible units vary in size from 40 m² (431 sq. ft.) studio flats to 120 m² (1,291 sq. ft.) apartments with galleries. Each unit has a no-partitions open plan design and perimeter structural walls. In the interiors, the architects used local materials such as wooden oak floors and granite tiled bathrooms.

The building is a splendid integration of old and new to create a unique composition that addresses contemporary needs.

1. Site plan. The project is located in the alpine area of Lake Bohinj with breathtaking views of the surrounding mountains. As a result, the organization of the housing and their façades is directed towards these views.
2–5. Floor plans. The flexible units vary in size and each unit has a no-partition open plan design and perimeter structural walls. In the interiors, the architects used local materials such as wooden oak floors and granite-tiled bathrooms.

pp. 176, 177
6. The stepped profile of the building traces the silhouette of the landscape in the background.
7. A cross section through the building showing the sloping roof.
8. The entrance lobby to the building.
9. The idea of transparency is omnipresent in the building through vertical wooden elements that form the balcony walls and façade panels.

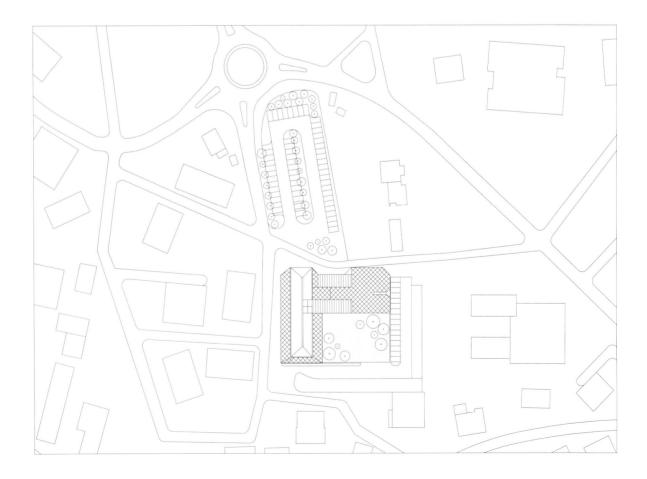

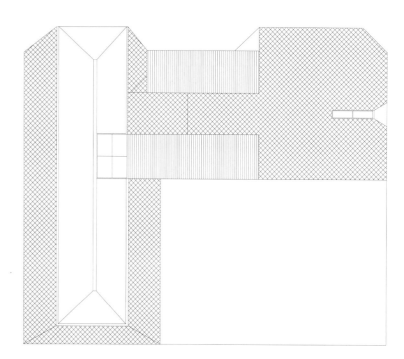

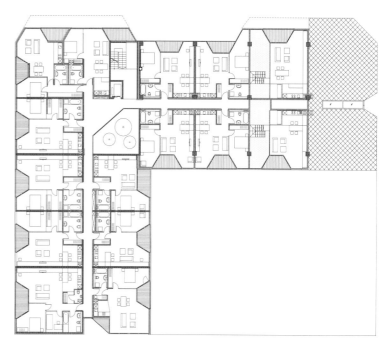

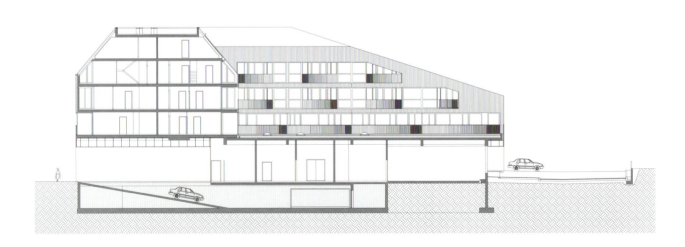

Tetris apartments, Ljubljana, Slovenia
Design: OFIS Arhitekti, 2007

The Tetris apartments building feature 650 flexible units on four storeys with a floor area of 5,000 m² (53,819 sq. ft.). Located on a relatively large site, the project was developed and then sold to the Slovenian Housing Fund which manages affordable housing for lower income families.

To avoid orientation towards a busy highway, the balconies of the structure that measure 58 m (190 ft.) long and 15 m (49 ft.) wide, were shifted at a 30 degrees angle towards the quieter south side. An interest to build two additional buildings along the longitudinal sides resulted in avoiding east or west facing windows. Some of the larger units feature a glazed loggia around the private balconies thereby privacy is created with no apartment having a direct view of another.

The flexible nature of these social housing units makes them available for purchase in many different sizes and arrangements. Their areas range from 30 m² (322 sq. ft.) studio flats up to three-room apartments of 70 m² (753 sq. ft.). The designers employed cost saving, quality materials in the interior of the larger apartments, including oak floors, granite tiled bathrooms, and large windows with external metal blinds.

The units were designed to be flexible and all the walls are non-structural. In regard to choice of materials, the inner façade's wall is made up of plaster and the external walls that form the loggia and are glazed or wrapped into precast panels. The balcony fences are either perforated precast panel or made of metal.

Ironically the name of the building was derived from its appearance. Many onlookers began to notice that the color scheme and forms employed along the façades resembled the popular Tetris game. In reality however, OFIS Arhitekti designed the façades simply by tracing the floor plans onto the elevations.

1. Site plan. To avoid orientation towards a busy highway, the balconies of the Tetris apartments were shifted at a 30-degree angle towards the quieter south side. An interest to build two additional buildings along the longitudinal sides resulted in avoiding east- or west-facing windows.

2–5. Floor plans. The flexible nature of these units makes them available for purchase in many different sizes and arrangements since all the walls are non-structural.

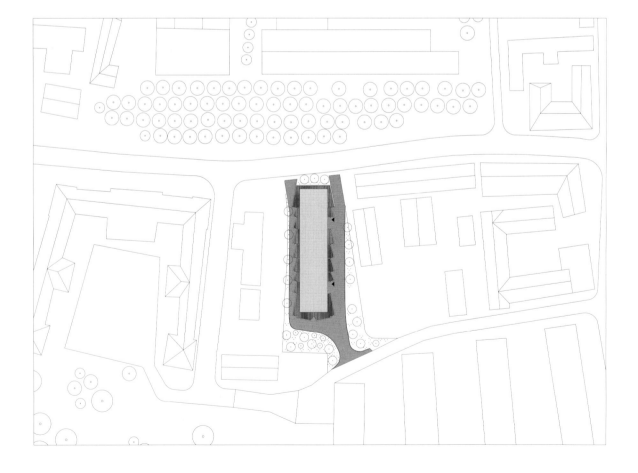

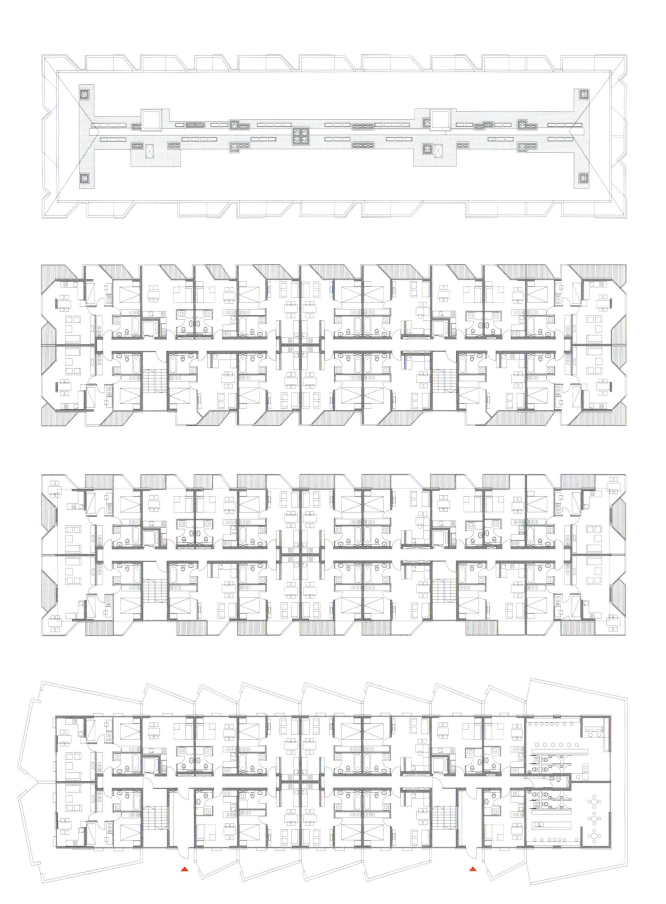

6. The building under construction.
7. Some of the larger units feature a glazed loggia around the private balconies thereby giving no apartment a direct view of another.
8. The external walls that form the loggia are glazed or wrapped into precast panels. The balcony fences are either perforated precast panel or made of metal.

VM houses, Copenhagen, Denmark
Design: BIG + JDS Architects, 2005

Built near Copenhagen, the VM houses is an apartment building that houses 230 flexible units on eight levels and a floor area of 25,000 m² (269,097 sq. ft.). When seen from above, this project appears as two structures shaped as a »V« and »M«.

The building was the first large project to be completed in Copenhagen's new Ørestad district that is linked to the city center via high speed public transit. Each block, can be regarded as a separate entity, but ultimately, they work very much in unison. The »V« building is located on one edge of the site's perimeter and is clearly defined by its four corners. The view of the neighboring structure was avoided by orientating it diagonally towards the vast open fields around. Along the south side of the »V« structure, the designers placed balconies that point outwards like rows of jagged shark's teeth. Each apartment has double-height ceilings to the north and vast panoramic views to the south. An exterior pathway leads to three stair and elevator towers to provide access to this wing. The diagonal slab utilized in the »V« building is broken down to smaller portions to form the »M« structure.

In the building's layout design, many ideas introduced in Le Corbusier's Unité d'habitation were revisited and improved on. For example, the central corridors connecting all apartments are short and receive abundance light from both ends. The individual terraces included in this segment are also on the south facing side while the rooftop terrace is accessible via a central corridor.

As the first residential complex in the area, the architects sought to create an inviting environment. To create exterior public space, they raised the »V« block 5 m (16.4 ft.) above ground and by placed it on columns. As a result, the courtyard is opened to the park along the southern façade. The architects also decomposed the façades with niches and angles to create a multitude of informal meeting spaces that encourage social interaction. The exterior of the »M« House is clad in floating panels of anodized aluminum.

The VM houses demonstrate that functionality and aesthetically pleasing ideas can go hand in hand.

1. When seen from above, the VM houses appear as two structures shaped as a »V« and »M«. The building was the first large project to be completed in Copenhagen's new Ørestad district.
2. The »V« building is located on one edge of the site's perimeter and is clearly defined by its four corners.

Floor 1

Room
12 M²

Partition screen

m2

m1

Room
24 M2

Shower
4 M2

Hallway
6 M2

Stairs

V/T

Shower
4 M.

Dining Room / Kitchen
38   M2

5 M²

Room
10 M.

Floor 2

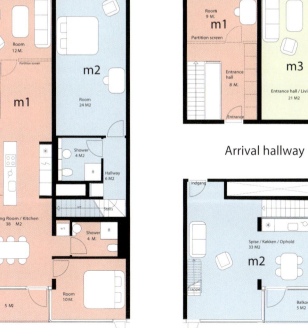

Room
9 M.

m1

Partition screen

Entrance
hall
8 M.

m3

Entrance hall / Living room
21 M2

Entrance

Arrival hallway

Indgang

Spise / Køkken / Ophold
33 M2

m2

Trappe

Balkon
5 M2

Floor 2

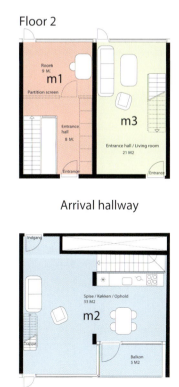

Room
9 M.

m1

Partition screen

Entrance
hall
8 M.

m3

Entrance hall / Living room
21 M2

Entrance

Arrival hallway

Indgang

Spise / Køkken / Ophold
33 M2

m2

Trappe

Balkon
5 M2

4–7. Floor plans (each apartment has double-height ceilings to the north and vast panoramic views to the south. An exterior pathway leads to three stair and elevator towers to provide access to this wing).
8. Along the south side of the »V«s structure, the designers placed balconies that point outwards like rows of jagged shark's teeth.
9, 10. The strikingly painted central corridors are short in length and receive abundant natural light from both ends.

Readings for the chapters' introductions

Historic evolution and contemporary trends effecting apartment buildings' design

French, H., *Key Urban Housing of the Twentieth Century: Plans, Sections and Elevations*, New York: W.W. Norton, 2008.

Friedman, A., *Town and Terraced Housing: For Affordability and Sustainability*, London: Routledge, 2011.

Schoenauer, N., *6000 years of housing*, New York: W.W. Norton, 2000.

Tafuri, M., and F. Dal Co, *Modern Architecture/1*. Milan: Electra Editrice, 1976.

Uffelen, C.V., *Apartment Buildings*, 1st ed., Berlin: Braun, 2013.

Net-zero buildings

Gevorkian, P., *Sustainable Energy Systems Engineering: The Complete Green Building Design Resource,* New York: McGraw Hill, 2007.

Gevorkian, P., *Alternative Energy Systems in Building Design*, New York: McGraw Hill, 2008.

Johnston, D., and S. Gibson, *Toward a Zero-Energy Home: A Complete Guide to Energy Self-Sufficiency at Home*, Newtown: Taunton Press, 2010.

Kruger, P., *Alternative Energy Resources: The Quest for Sustainable Energy*, Hoboken: John Wiley & Sons, Inc., 2006.

Minkel, J.R., »The 2003 Northeast Blackout – Five Years Later: Tougher regulatory measures are in place, but we're still a long way from a ›smart‹ power grid«, *Scientific American*, August 13, 2008, p. 11.

Voss, K., and E. Musall, *Net-Zero Energy Buildings: International Projects of Carbon Neutrality in Buildings*, Bergische Universität Wuppertal, 2013.

Mixed-use buildings

Al-Kodmany, K., »Placemaking with Tall Buildings«, *Urban Design International*, vol. 16, issue 4, September, 2011, pp. 252–269.

Coupland, A., *Reclaiming the City: Mixed Use Development*, London: E & FN Spon, 1997.

Feehan, D., and D.F. Marvin, *Making Business Districts Work: Leadership and Management of Downtown, Main Street, Business District, and Community Development of Organizations, New York*: Haworth Press, 2006.

Grant, J., »*Encouraging Mixed Use in Practice*«, *Paper prepared for: International Planning Symposium on Incentives, Regulations, and Plans – The Role of States and Nation-States in Smart Growth Planning*, 2004.

Kim, Y., L. Jolly, A. Fairhurst, and A. Kelly, »Mixed-Use Development: Creating a Model of Key Success Factors«, *Journal of Shopping Center Research*, vol. 12, issue 1, 2005.

Schwanke, D., *Mixed-Use Development Handbook*, Washington, D.C., Urban Land Institute, 2003.

Tombari, A.E., *Smart Growth Smart Choices Series: Mixed Use Development, National Association of Home Builders (NAHB)*, Land Development Services, Washington, D.C., 2006.

Creative open and meeting spaces in buildings

Marcus, C., »Shared Open Space and Community Life«, *Place*, vol. 15, no. 2, Winter, 2003.

Marcus, C., and W. Sarkissian, *Housing as If People Mattered: Site Design Guidelines for Medium-Density Family Housing*, Berkeley: University of California Press, 1986.

Piedmont-Palladino, M., *Green Community*, Chicago: American Planning Association, 2009.

Converting old structures to contemporary residential use

Jokilehto, J., *A History of Architectural Conservation*, Oxford: Butterworth Heinemann, 1999.

Moudon, A.V., *Built for Change: Neighborhood Architecture in San Francisco*, Cambridge: MIT Press, 1986.

Osborne, B.S., »Landscapes, memory, monuments, and commemoration: Putting identity in its place«, *Canadian Ethnic Studies*, vol. 33 (3), pp. 39–77, 2001.

Ouf, A., »Authenticity and the Sense of Place in Urban Design«, *Journal of Urban Design*, vol. 6 (1). pp. 73–86, 2001.

Unique building methods and materials

Calkins, M., *Materials for Sustainable Sites: A Complete Guide to the Evaluation, Selection, and Use of Sustainable Construction Materials*, Hoboken: John Wiley & Sons, 2009.

Fernandez, J., *Material Architecture: Emergent Materials for Innovative Buildings and Ecological Considerations*, Amsterdam: Elsevier, 2006.

Hegger, M., et al., *Construction Materials Manual*, Basel, Boston, and Berlin: Birkhäuser, 2006.

Keeler, M., and B. Burke, *Fundamentals of Integrated Design for Sustainable Building*, Hoboken: John Wiley & Sons, Inc., 2009.

Sassi, P., *Strategies for Sustainable Architecture*, Abingdon and New York: Taylor and Francis, 2006.

»Social Housing Tower of 75 Units In Europa Square / Roldán + Berengué«, 25 Apr. 2011. *Arch-Daily*. Accessed 16 Mar. 2016. <http://www.archdaily.com/130267/social-housing-tower-of-75-units-in-europa-square-roldan-berengue/>

Yudelson, J., *Green Building A to Z: Understanding the Language of Green Building. Gabriola Island*, New Society Publishers, 2007.

Apartments for seniors and multigenerational arrangements

Calkins, M. P., »Powell Lawton's Contributions to Long Term care Settings«, *Journal of Housing for the Elderly*, vol. 17(1/2), pp. 67–84, 2003.

Lawlor, D. and M. A. Thomas, *Residential Design for Aging in Place*, Hoboken: John Wiley & Sons, 2008.

Nichols, A., »Tackling Dementia and Alzheimer's; The Future is in Your DNA«, *Focus Medicine*, McGill University, Montreal: Spring Issue, 2011.

Preiser, W. F. E., and E. Ostroff, *Universal Design Handbook*, New York & Toronto: McGraw-Hill, 2001.

Regnier, V. Powell Lawton's Contributions to Purpose-Built Housing Design for the Elderly. *Journal for Housing for the Elderly*, vol. 17 (1/2), pp. 39–54, 2003.

Buildings with sustainable technologies

Dunnett, N., and N. Kingsbury, *Planting Green Roofs and Living Walls*, Portland & Cambridge: Timber Press, 2008.

Fuad-Luke, A., *The Eco-Design Handbook*, London: Thames & Hudson, 2004.

Harvey, D., *A Handbook on Low-Energy Buildings and District-Energy Systems*; *Fundamentals, Techniques, and Examples*, London and Sterling: Earthscan, 2003.

Johnston, D., and S. Gibson, *Green from the Ground Up: Sustainable, Healthy, and Energy-Efficient Home Construction*, Newtown: The Taunton Press, 2008.

Keeler, M., and B. Burke, *Fundamentals of Integrated Design for Sustainable Building*, Hoboken: John Wily & Sons, Inc., 2009.

Kwok, A., and W. Grondzik, *The Green Studio Handbook: Environmental Strategies for Schematic Design*, Amsterdam: Elsevier Architectural Press, 2007.

Snodgrass, E. and L. McIntyre, *The Green Roof Manual*, London: The Timber Press, 2010.

Strongman, C., *The Sustainable Home: The Essential Guide to Eco Building, Renovation and Decoration*, London: Merrell Publishers, 2008.

Designing for live-work arrangements

Becker, F., and F. Steele, *Workplace by Design*, San Francisco: Jossey-Bass Inc., 1995.

Dietsch, D. K., *Live/Work: Working at Home, Living at Work*, Singapore: Abrams, 2008.

Hascher, R, S. Jeska and B. Klauck, eds. *A Design Manual: Office Buildings*, Basel: Birkhäuser, 2002.

Penn, M., *Microtrends: Suprising Tales of the Way We Live Today*, London: Penguin, 2008

Swenson, R., *The Overload Syndrome: Learning To Live Within Your Limits*, Colorado Springs: NavPress, 1998.

Buildings with flexible interiors and micro units

Broto, C., *Small Houses*, Barcelona: Broto, 2007.

Burney, T., »Good Things Come in Small Packages«, *Builder Magazine*, February, 2010.

Losantos, A., *Mini House Now*, New York: Harper Design, 2006.

Conran, T., *How to Live in Small Spaces*, New York: Firefly Books, 2007.

Gauer, J., *The New American Dream: Living Well in Small Homes*, New York: Monacelli Press, 2004.

Photo credits

Iwan Baan 49.6, 108.5, 141.7, 141.8
Helene Binet 160.1, 161.2
Luc Boegly 18.1, 20.5, 21.7
Bœlgen 111.2, 113.8
Zooey Braun 152.6, 152.7, 153.8, 153.9
Scott Burrows 157.2, 158.3, 159.6
J. Collingridge 61.5, 62.6, 63.7, 63.8
Peter Cook 84.6, 85.7
Johan Fowelin 183.2
David Franck 6, 56.1, 58.4, 58.5, 59.6
Avi Friedman 9.1, 10.2, 11.3, 11.4, 12.5, 13.6, 53.3,
    53.4, 54.5, 55.9
Shai Gil 69.9, 69.10
Sergio Grazia 12.2, 17.8
Tomaz Gregoric 176.6, 177.8, 177.9, 180.6, 180.8,
    180.9
Shu He 47.3, 48.4
Edward Hendricks 81.6, 81.7
Hertha Hurnaus 172.8, 172.9, 173.10, 173.11,
    173.12, 173.13
Barbara Karant 146.1, 147.2
Alan Karchmer 70.1, 71.4, 72.5, 73.6, 73.7
Yong-Kwan Kim 166.5, 167.6, 167.7
Carsten Kring 108.4
Dale Christopher Lang 40.1, 42.5, 43.6, 43.7
Rita Lehoux 142.1, 144.3, 145.5
Jens Lindhe 13.6, 107.2, 139.2, 140.4
Adam Mørk 92.1, 93.3, 93.4, 94.6, 95.10
Jaime Navarro 2, 74.2, 76.8, 77.9
Scott Norsworthy 67.2, 68.3
Jesse Ramirez 133.2, 133.3, 134.4, 135.5, 135.6
Mike Rebholz 148.4, 149.5
Brian Rose 120.1, 121.2, 122.6, 123.7
Cécile Septet 88.1, 90.5, 90.6, 91.7
Jordi Surroca 114.1, 116.5, 117.6
Jeffrey Totaro 129.3, 130.6, 131.7, 131.8
Romina Tonucci 144.4
Koichi Torimura 22.1, 23.3, 25.7
Steve Troes 26.1, 28.7, 29.8, 29.9
Julian Weyer 96.1, 97.4, 98.5, 99.6
Christiane Wirth 125.2, 126.4
Batár Zsolt 103.6, 104.7, 105.8, 105.9